A KITE IN A HURRICANE NO MORE

A KITE IN A HURRICANE NO MORE

The Journey of One Young Woman Who Overcame Learning Disabilities through Science and Educational Choice

By Mia Giordano and Lance Izumi

PRI PACIFIC RESEARCH INSTITUTE

A Kite in a Hurricane No More: The Journey of One Young Woman Who Overcame Learning Disabilities through Science and Educational Choice by Mia Giordano and Lance Izumi

November 2020

ISBN: 978-1-934276-43-3

Pacific Research Institute
PO Box 60485
Pasadena, CA 91116
Tel: 415-989-0833
www.pacificresearch.org

For Christine Zanello, whose love for her daughter and whose dedication in improving the learning for her child and to raising the quality of education for all children is an inspiration.

CONTENTS

INTRODUCTION
Lance Izumi

The title of this book is *A Kite in A Hurricane No More,* and between the covers you will find three different stories that intertwine to form a larger narrative that is much more expansive and larger in scope than what one would find in a typical autobiography.

The first is the autobiographical story of the life, challenges, perseverance, and ultimate triumph of Mia Giordano. She grew up with serious learning disabilities which appeared to sentence her to a life of futility, disappointment, and sadness.

Conventional schools could not address Mia's problems effectively but the ability of her parents to choose a non-conventional education path that met her needs resulted in a life-changing metamorphosis for Mia. This journey holds lessons for policymakers, parents, and the public alike.

The second story is a journey into the world of science and the mysteries of the brain. Advances in research show that the brain, far from being a static unchanging organ, is actually changeable and ever changing.

Yet, the paradigm used by policymakers and school officials to address the needs of children with learning disabilities has largely failed to take note of this new research and has thus failed to change in order to best address the needs of those like Mia who struggle with such disabilities.

There are proven learning programs, however, that do incorporate the latest brain research into their education practices, and Mia was the beneficiary of one such program. The story behind the creation of that program is just as fascinating as the new brain research itself.

Equity demands that the education options that have been available to Mia should also be available to the millions of other children who would benefit from greater school choice.

Finally, the third story is about public policy and why parents need to have educational choice options that meet the needs of their children.

Mia is special for many reasons, including the fact that she attended both public and private schools, had been home-schooled, and currently attends a charter high school. School choice has been a key to her life success, as it has been for so many children across the country.

Equity demands that the education options that have been available to Mia should also be available to the millions of other children who would benefit from greater school choice. Thankfully, there are proven programs in various states that can serve as models for providing such choice and equity.

These three stories will alternate in the chapter structure of this book, with Mia's autobiography alternating with chapters on brain science and educational policy. In the end, these intertwined stories converge to tell a larger and greater story of what the future of education in America could and should be.

CHAPTER ONE
Before the Beginning
Mia Giordano

My grandma used to tell me how I would make sure everybody was okay before myself. I would go around and ask everyone if they were okay and do you need something. She said I was very considerate, and I always thought about people before myself. Yeah, she thought I would be a social worker!

When I think back on my grandma's memory from my early childhood, initially I smile, but when I really think about it I realize how we never know how life will twist and turn. How could I have known in a few short years, I would be the one asking for help because I was not okay.

However, I am getting ahead of myself. Who is this young woman who is about to tell her story of tears and joys, of despair and triumph?

While writing this book I would listen to music. I love classical music, especially ballet. One of my favorite ballets is *Swan*

Lake, and before the ballet's first act there is a prologue that sets up the beautiful and emotional story to come. So, here is my prologue to the different acts of my life.

On my mom's side of the family, her paternal grandparents were born in Italy and came to the United States at the start of the Great Depression. They had very humble backgrounds. In fact, they were virtually penniless when they came to America.

My great grandmother only spoke Italian but taught herself to speak and write English. She was a great seamstress and like many other female immigrants at that time, worked in one of the garment factories in San Francisco, where they had settled.

They saved their money and eventually opened a bakery called Stella Pastry in the Little Italy part of San Francisco in 1942. Stella is still there today, although our family no longer owns it. It is known for its traditional Italian pastries and cakes. Stella's specialty is Sacripantina, which combines layers of vanilla sponge cake, rum and Italian custard called zabaglione. It is so delicious!

My great grandparents created and lived their own American dream. The bakery was a success and they were able to buy their own home. They had two children, my grandfather and his younger sister. Being good Italian Catholics, they sent their children to Catholic school. Both went to college and my grandfather earned a master's degree.

My grandfather met my grandmother at a wedding. She was so gorgeous that all the guys were too scared to ask her to dance. Except for my grandfather. He was a good dancer, asked her to dance, and told her that he was going to marry her. She gave a good sharp Italian reply: "You're crazy!"

My grandfather persevered. He dated her for two years and then they got married. So, there is a history of doing the impossible in my family.

My grandmother is an intelligent woman, who was on the forefront of the early computer programming for Hewlett Packard at the time when there were very few women in the computer industry.

My grandfather got his real estate license and became a very successful developer building important projects in San Francisco.

My mom, Christine, is the only child of my grandparents and she is my best friend. She's a lawyer, but decided practicing law was not for her.

Well, my mom found something a lot better. She became executive director of the Make-A-Wish Foundation Greater Bay Area. The foundation is famous for granting wishes for children suffering from critical illnesses. When my mom took over the foundation, she had lots of volunteers, but insufficient funds to support the wish-granting program. She turned things around and the foundation was soon granting a wish a day to seriously ill kids.

My mom talks about the incredible and inspiring stories of the children she met and helped. She said that the greatest gift to a child is the possibility of a miracle. Little did she know that because of her love and commitment to me she would give me the miracle of learning, a life of opportunities and endless possibilities.

On my father's side of the family, his mother was of German, Irish, and English descent, while his father was Italian.

My father, Stephen, is the younger of five children in his family. His father was a firefighter in Burlingame, a city just south of San Francisco. His mother was a homemaker.

My father is a contractor and my mother calls him the Giorgio Armani of concrete construction. Like Armani, he was an innovator, who could make stamped concrete look like fine tapestry.

My mom and dad both attended Burlingame High School. Years later, one of my dad's friends ran into my mom. This friend immediately contacted my dad to tell him that my mom was single. It did not take my dad long to get in touch with my mom. They dated and the rest is history. They got married in 2001.

In 2002, I came along and my story really began.

CHAPTER TWO
It Begins
Mia Giordano

Even when I was a baby, I wanted to learn.

My mom always tells me that I would look at people's mouths to study and analyze the movements as they were talking. That study must have paid off because I began to speak very early on.

In fact, I was ahead of the game in a lot of areas. I started crawling very early and I started walking at a very early age.

My sister Cara was born 15 months after me. I love my sister so much! When I was small, I could not pronounce her name. So, I would just tell people, "that's my baby, Car Car!"

Like a good Italian, I have always loved to eat and I still do. When I was little, my mom would turn on the television to the Food Network and I would watch endless cooking shows. Cartoons were great, but food is better.

One of my favorite activities was drawing. My mom likes to tell the story of the time she was on the phone and out of the corner of her eye she saw me running. She looked around and saw that I had a Sharpie marker pen in my hand with the cap off. To her horror, I was squealing and laughing as I drew a bold line across the wall, the dresser, and then a beautiful silk lampshade. Afterwards, I got a lesson on the important uses of paper. I would recite: "Not on the walls, only on the paper!"

Throughout my life I have always made friends very easily. I remember being on a family vacation when I was just four or five, and making friends with a group of other five-year-olds and leading them on an adventure in a clubhouse. We had a great time, but I did not just want to play with other kids, I really wanted to get to know them. So, I always asked a lot of questions, that way I learned everything I could about my new friends.

My love for nature comes from my early childhood as well. My mom would take my sister and me on walks where we would look at all the flowers and plants. She would explain to us the names of the flowers and have us touch them.

Ever since I can remember I have been very outgoing and expressive. On Christmas Eve, we would have an open house inviting our friends and family. The invitation always read: "Come solo or with a crowd. All are welcome." Usually we had more than a hundred people.

As a little girl, I would tell everyone a story. Looking back, my stories were quite elaborate for a small child, with a beginning, middle, and an ending. For example, one of my stories was about The Flying Dutchman, the legendary ghost ship. My relatives evidently liked my stories, so it became a family tradition for me to tell a story at our Christmas gatherings.

I have already mentioned that I liked classical music and ballet. One year, my mom took me to see the ballet *Romeo and Juliet*. Of course, sadly, in the end Romeo and Juliet die. That ending made me very angry, and I scolded my mom, "Mama, that was a really baaaad ending!"

So, I had a wonderful early childhood, with lots of love, lots of great memories and lots of loving people.

My mom says my learning development seemed to be normal. She enrolled me in a Montessori preschool when I was three. Montessori education focuses on the child and believes that children are naturally eager to learn. Even though I was quite young, I remember playing and enjoying preschool.

At Montessori preschool, you would do things called jobs. So, for example, you could be working on stringing beads for a necklace. You take the materials from the proper tray and when you are finished you put things back on the tray. I was very good at doing jobs.

At preschool, I was able to pick up the sounds of the alphabet. My mom read lots of books to me and I liked to read. I especially enjoyed the *Curious George* books and Bible stories like David and Goliath and The Last Supper.

Everything seemed to be going fine. I was having a happy normal early childhood and I seemed to be doing well in preschool.

But then the first indication of trouble popped up.

I started to have problems breathing. My mom noticed it. My teacher at preschool also noticed it. In fact, my teacher told my mom that I sounded like Darth Vader because I was breathing so hard.

The problem was centered in my head. I felt like I was always clogged up and it was really hard to breathe through my nose. I ended up having to breathe through my mouth a lot.

I started to snore, too. I would literally stop breathing for moments during my sleep, which, of course, disturbed my ability to get a good night's sleep.

My mom became worried and took me to see a pediatrician when I was four. The doctor focused on my tonsils, which were enlarged but not infected. He didn't take my tonsils out and said that my mouth breathing and snoring would eventually go away.

He asked my mom if I was falling asleep in class. I was not, but I was always excited, and it turns out that when kids have broken sleep they can become excitable.

The advice was we could just wait and see, and there was probably nothing to worry about. Unfortunately, as time would tell, there was a lot to worry about.

CHAPTER THREE

How the Brain Works and How to Change It
Lance Izumi

I, too, could make no sense of the relationship between the big and little hands of an analogue clock. Asked to perform the simple addition of a two-digit column of numbers, I would randomly choose numbers from the left or right side. The logic of basic math, the concept of telling time, the ability to truly comprehend what I was hearing or reading: all eluded me. On the playground, I couldn't follow conversations or the rules of simple games.

—Barbara Arrowsmith-Young,
   The Woman Who Changed Her Brain[1]

The Arrowsmith Program is the brainchild, both literally and figuratively, of Canada's Barbara Arrowsmith-Young, who received her graduate degree in school psychology from the University of Toronto. As a child and young adult, she recalled, "I lived in a dense fog," where the fog was not the cold Canadian weather, but a fog clouding her brain and mind.[2]

In order to understand Arrowsmith-Young's brain fog and the fog that would come to afflict Mia, one must first understand how the brain works and what the relationship is between learning dysfunctions and weaknesses in parts of the brain. With that understanding, one can then see the logic in the Arrowsmith program, which would eventually change Mia's life, and then fairly evaluate its effectiveness.

THE BRAIN

According to the early 20th Century German anatomist Korbinian Brodmann, there are 52 distinct areas of the brain. Each area is different from one another based on their cellular makeup. For instance, area 17 is the primary visual cortex, while 41 and 42 are the primary auditory areas.[3] These Brodmann areas are still in use today.

"Each of these brain areas has its own particular function," notes Arrowsmith-Young, and points out that area 6 "in the left hemisphere, the premotor region, is responsible for the conversion of individual motor impulses into smoothly and consecutively organized skilled movement." This skilled movement "consists of a series of consecutive links between motor impulses requiring smooth changes from one link of the series to another."[4]

Examples of smooth and consecutively organized skilled movements include writing out the alphabet and "the smooth, automatized performance of an arithmetic procedure requiring the use of a complex sequential chain of elements."[5]

It is crucial to understand, however, that these brain areas do not operate in isolation. Rather, she notes that complex mental and behavioral processes, such as speaking, reading, and writing, are the result of the interaction of these brain areas and that each area makes its own contributions to the dynamic whole or functional system.[6]

Citing the pioneering Russian scientist A.R. Luria, Arrowsmith-Young says that a functional system "is a group of brain areas working together to carry out a specific higher mental process to which each component brain area makes its own particular contribution according to its own individual characteristic of mental functioning or activity."[7]

Dr. Greg Rose, a professor in the department of anatomy and physiology at Southern Illinois University who is one of the nation's leading neuroscientists, says "it turns out that there are networks in the brain, different brain regions that can be physically separated from each other, that synchronize their activity."

"So, they work together," he explains, "and the idea is that they will be doing this and you can observe this even when the brain is at idle."

Thus, for instance, according to a University of British Columbia study, research "points to the importance of a functional connection between the neuroanatomical areas associated with language cognition and motor functioning in reading."[8]

So, the different parts of the brain are interconnected to make a functioning whole. What happens, then, if there are problems in different parts of the brain?

LEARNING DYSFUNCTIONS AND BRAIN WEAKNESSES

Because the brain areas are interconnected, problems in any area of the brain will cause a domino effect:

> A problem in any one brain area will affect higher mental processes in a particular way depending on the mental operations or activi-

ties carried out by that specific brain area in its contribution to the functional system. Since the same brain area may be a component of several different functional systems "the presence of a primary defect, interfering with the proper function of a given part of the brain, inevitably leads to disturbances of a group of functional systems."[9]

So, if there is a problem in area 6, which, recall, is the area of the premotor region responsible for the conversion of individual motor impulses into smoothly and consecutively organized skilled movement, then skilled writing movements could be replaced by isolated writing of individual letters, with the person writing the letters over and over again.[10]

But a problem in area 6 would not only cause writing impairment. Problems in that area of the brain would also cause impairments in speaking and carrying out arithmetic operations: "Thus, each of these three functional systems (writing, speaking, and arithmetic) is disturbed in the same characteristic way when there is damage to the premotor zone."[11]

In other words, a problem in an area of the brain will cause learning disabilities or dysfunctions. According to University of British Columbia researchers: "In general, children and youth with [learning disabilities] are found to have disrupted, altered, and/or less effective connections between crucial brain areas that form the neural networks supporting academic skill learning and demonstration."[12]

Citing the work of the Russian scientist Luria, Arrowsmith-Young notes, "mental processes which on the surface seem to have nothing in common are actually related through dependences on a particular brain area."

So, "performing mathematical operations, understanding logical grammatical structures and naming objects do not appear to have anything in common, yet all of these processes are adversely affected by the same lesion to the parieto-temporo-occipital zone in the left hemisphere." The result is "a disturbance in the analysis and understanding of symbolic relationships." In concrete terms:

> In arithmetic there is a disintegration of the categorical structure of number and of the system of mathematical relationships (e.g., the number one thousand and twenty four could be written as 1024 or 1000 24; there would be difficulty differentiating between symmetrical numbers 17-71; in adding 17+25, it could become 1+7+2+5). There is difficulty in comprehending any construction that involves logical grammatical relationships (e.g., brother's father and father's brother; Kate is younger than Mary, but older than Jenny. Who is oldest?). Naming objects becomes difficult because the system of semantic relationships built up around the word which gives that word its specific meaning have been disrupted. In all cases there is a difficulty in simultaneous integration of separate symbolic elements into a unified whole and the understanding of their relationship.[13]

Therefore, "a specific brain area that is weaker in functioning, for whatever reason, than the person's remaining brain areas such that it significantly impairs the mental activities of the functional systems in which it is involved" will cause a learning dysfunction.[14]

Given that weak areas of the brain will cause learning dysfunctions, what can be done to help people overcome their learning dysfunctions? That question will be answered in Chapter Five.

CHAPTER FOUR
Kindergarten is No Walk in the Garden and Then Things Get Worse
Mia Giordano

Things had gone well at my Montessori preschool, so there was not a lot of concern for my parents about how things would go for me when I entered kindergarten.

My family lives in the town of Hillsborough, south of San Francisco. My mom had gone to North School, a public elementary school in Hillsborough. She enjoyed it. Therefore, she was confident when she enrolled me in the full-day kindergarten.

However, she had immediate concerns after attending a parent meeting just before the school year started.

During that meeting, the parents were informed that their kids were going to come home tired and cranky. The school had a rigorous academic program and the children would be required to complete quite a load of homework and various additional activities.

My mom had a bad feeling in the pit of her stomach. She told me later she raised her hand and asked why should a five-year-old be doing homework after going through a whole day at kindergarten. She also asked if there was any evidence that homework for such young children was actually helpful.

In the end, though, her questions did not go over well with those leading the meeting.

Afterwards, other parents who attended the meeting came up to her and told her that they were wondering the same thing. But everyone was stuck. Their kids would all be going into that school, no matter the doubts they had. Including me.

It turned out that my mom's worries were justified. I had a terrible time in kindergarten at that school.

The school had been truthful—there was a lot of homework every day. As a five-year-old, I just wanted to play, watch some TV, eat dinner, and go to bed. The heavy homework burden was hard on me at that age.

Things had gone well at my Montessori preschool, so there was not a lot of concern about how things would go for me when I entered kindergarten.

Worse than the homework load, though, was my time in the classroom. The school had very strict rules. If you violated those rules, you would get a colored card. Up to that point, I had never had any behavior problems in my young life. In fact, my mom always reminded me that I never even went through the "terrible twos."

During some classroom activity, however, I was looking at my nails and fidgeting. All of the sudden, the teacher hands me a yellow card, which meant that you did something that you were not supposed to do. I had no idea what I did wrong. I went home in tears.

The principal told my mom that I was perhaps a gifted child and that might be the reason for the issues I had been having at the school. This suggestion caused my mom to have me tested.

I took the WPPSI-III, which measures a broad range of subjects. The test results put me at the 99th percentile. The only area where I didn't score at that level was in processing speed, which was an indication of my troubles to come.

Despite those high test scores, the fact remained that I was just miserable at that school. Even though I was supposedly gifted, the principal said that the school did not have any extra funds to meet the needs of gifted students.

By Thanksgiving, it was clear that it was time for a change. I was pulled out of the public school and put back in my old Montessori school.

I was so happy. On the first day back at the Montessori school I ran up the stairs of the school, looked back and waved at my mom, and felt completely at home.

While the return to the Montessori school was a great choice for me, my health was still declining. By the end of my kindergarten year, I was having real problems breathing.

It felt like I had two big cotton balls under the upper bridge of my nose and that air was going through this thick filter. I felt like I could not get enough oxygen, so I was always breathing through my mouth.

At night in bed, my breathing only seemed to get worse. Not only was my snoring getting louder, I would lurch up into a sitting position with my neck stretched out as far as it could go. I just remember gasping for air.

My mom, who had been reading up on the brain, was worried that I was going to suffer brain damage because of my breathing issues. The doctor, though, kept saying that things would get better and I would grow out of it.

Unfortunately, not only would things not get better, my breathing problems started to affect my learning.

Even though I had tested at these high levels, I started to have trouble reading. In particular, I was beginning to have problems with what is called phonological and phonemic awareness.

The most common definition of phonological awareness is a skill that allows a person to identify and manipulate parts of oral language such as words and syllables. Phonemic awareness is the ability to hear, identify, and manipulate individual sounds, which are called phonemes, in spoken words. In order to read, children need to be aware of how sounds in words work together.[15]

For example, the word "cat" has three phonemes: /c/ /a/ /t/. There are 44 phonemes in English, and phonemic awareness is the foundation for spelling and word recognition.

At first, my reading problems fell under the radar and did not send up a red flag. However, by the end of kindergarten, I was beginning to experience problems with instructions. I would hear the first part of instructions, but I would not hear the second or third part.

I was like a ship that looked fine above the water line but had some little holes just below the surface. In time, those holes would only get bigger. As I entered the first grade the academics and learning would get more serious and the holes would become more apparent.

As much as I liked the Montessori school, I was accepted to attend first grade at the Phillips Brooks School, which is a private elementary school in the town of Menlo Park, south of San Francisco. The school has a great academic reputation, but would it be a good fit for me? The answer was "no."

There is a leap in difficulty from kindergarten to the first grade. The reading is based on phonological and phonemic awareness, and you learn to read more complex sentences and be able to handle multiple-step directions. This increase in difficulty led to some real problems for me.

I remember a lesson where we were given four cards and we had to put the four cards together to make a logical storyline. I just could not figure out how to put those cards together to make a complete story that could be understood.

In addition, I began to have a difficult time understanding what I was reading. I could not understand what the story was about. And it was not just books.

I had a difficult time understanding the movies. For example, one of my favorite movies at that time was "Bee Movie," with Jerry Seinfeld and Renée Zellweger as the voices for the two bees. I really loved that movie and thought it was hilarious. However, I had trouble following the plot, what the bees were discussing, and what they were trying to fix in their world. I really felt like I was getting half the story, and those problems stemmed from my learning issues, not from bad Hollywood scriptwriters.

I was like a ship that looked fine above the water line but had some little holes just below the surface. Those holes would only get bigger.

Another area that was a real challenge for me was handwriting. I had a serious problem connecting the letters and words I was seeing and then writing them down on paper. There seemed to be this disconnect between what I was seeing in my brain and the communication to my hand to write it down. I could eventually do it, but it would take me a lot longer than other kids in my class.

Not only was there this disconnect between my brain and my hand, I also could not stay within the lines of the writing paper. My writing was all over the place. As time went on, my writing got to be more like abstract art.

My mom also started to notice things at home. For example, she noticed that I was having problems with taking directions. If she told me to do four different things, I would not get the fourth thing.

By the end of the first grade, I was having a lot of learning issues and my health issues were getting worse. So my mom took me to see a pediatric ENT/sleep specialist. She had made a video of me sleeping and as soon as the doctor watched it, he diagnosed me with sleep apnea.

Sleep apnea occurs when someone repeatedly stops and starts breathing during sleep. Loud snoring and gasping for air, which I had, are signs of sleep apnea.

Between the first and second grade, I had surgery. The doctor went inside my nasal cavity and used a laser to remove obstructions to my airway. My tonsils and adenoids were also removed. After that, I could breathe normally, but the doctor said that it would take a year for me to heal fully from the surgery.

Even though the operation had eliminated my sleep apnea, I still did not realize fully the damage that had been done to my brain.

Even though the operation had eliminated my sleep apnea, I still did not realize fully the damage that had been done to my brain.

I did not know that scientists had found that sleep apnea can cause progressive brain damage. Apnea changes the chemicals in the brain and scrambles how the brain works.[16]

Understanding my brain damage would have to wait for a while. When I entered the second grade, I just wanted to cope.

In order to help me cope, my family arranged for me to have reading tutoring that used the Slingerland method. The Slingerland approach helps kids with reading problems, especially dyslexic children. Even though I was not dyslexic, I was certainly having problems with reading.

The Slingerland organization says that their method starts with the smallest unit of sight, sound, and feel—a single letter—and then builds on that single letter to enable "the strong channel of learning to reinforce the weak." So, "From single letters, students are taught how to associate sounds with their visual counterparts and put these letters together to spell words."[17]

What I remember is that the Slingerland tutoring I received did help me. However, that help did not address the weakness that had developed in my brain. It helped me compensate for my weakness, but it did not eliminate my weakness. In reality, it helped me temporarily, but it was not sustainable.

In the second grade, the school told my mom, basically, that I had a learning disability and that she and I had to live with it. Even at that time my mom knew that brains are not static and that they can change for the better, so she was incensed by that judgment.

> **What I remember is that the Slingerland tutoring I received did help me. However, that help did not address the weakness that had developed in my brain.**

Still, I went to school and I was mostly able to fly under the radar in the second grade. I say "mostly" because the school had implied that I was suffering from attention deficit hyperactivity disorder, or ADHD. My mom had me tested for ADHD and the results showed that I was not suffering from that condition. Also, the school said I had to meet certain academic milestones or else I would not be able to continue as a student there.

So, my family arranged for me to receive help from a Slingerland specialist named Jennifer, who was also a speech pathologist. To this day Jennifer remains a close and revered friend. I also had a math specialist while I was in school. I was able to read, but I was still sounding out words. I was also using pictures in books to help me understand what the reading was about. Again, I was using compensating strategies.

Despite my challenges, I worked very hard. I wanted to do well and learn. Because I had these problems, my mom said that I worked harder than the other kids in my class and she said that it made me stronger.

But as my mom also said, all these strategies we were using just "put a Band-Aid on the problem."

In the third grade, things came crashing down. The reading in the third grade was harder. We did not have books with lots of pictures, so I could not use pictures to help me visually to understand the reading. I was having a tough time putting words together to make sense of them.

I also started stuttering badly. It was hard for me to spit out words and put them into a sentence. As I would try to sound out words I would stutter. When I would start to stutter, I would then just shut down. It was around that time that the movie "The King's Speech" came out, which told the story of King George VI and his stutter. I was like the king. What a way to be like royalty.

I had always had difficulty with math, but in the third grade I had a lot of problems. I could not do multiplication or division well. For example, I remember taking a timed multiplication test, having to complete 30 problems in five minutes. I had memorized the multiplication tables, but I could not get that information from my brain onto the paper and write my answers quickly. It took me a long time to process the problem and get the answer out. Of course, I did not do well on that test.

In general, I felt like I was going in slow motion and everybody else was going at lightning speed.

When my teacher wrote something on the board, I had difficulty. I would usually ask one of my classmates to tell me what it said and then repeat it to me, which would allow me to understand what was written.

Sadly, my learning problems caused some of my classmates to make fun of me. To this day, those painful memories make me cry.

When the teacher would say something in class, I would often have to ask her to repeat what she had just said. Many of my classmates would then heave up a very loud sigh.

Many of the kids in class started to stay away from me, which made me feel lonely. In fact, the school called up my mom one time to say that I was apart from my classmates, just all by myself, and that I was very sad. I started to be more isolated.

There was one especially sad episode. A girl in school made up a song about me with the words: "Mia is dumb, dumb, dumb." It made me sad at the time, but looking back it made me stronger.

The school also informed my mom that I was suffering from depression, which I was not. My pediatrician wrote a letter to the school saying that I did not have depression and I was happy at home. Again, it was frustrating and infuriating that my school would say these things about me that were simply ridiculous.

With things going downhill fast, the school sent a letter to my family in November of my third grade year saying that I was not going to be invited back for the fourth grade. That seemed like a turkey of a Thanksgiving present, but God works in mysterious ways.

If the school had not asked me to leave, I would never have found the Arrowsmith Program, which totally changed my life.

CHAPTER FIVE
The Arrowsmith Program
Lance Izumi

When she was a young woman, Barbara Arrowsmith-Young recalls being in graduate school where she was studying psychology. Because of her learning disabilities, which had never been addressed, her life was a nightmare.

"I was working 20 hours a day, seven days a week, sleeping four hours a night," she recalls, "and that that was just to get through and to get by." She had no social relations, did not understand people, and did not understand why things happened, so she became very socially isolated.

Not surprisingly, she also struggled academically.

"I saw other students," she remembers, "and they could read an article maybe once or twice, get the concept and then be able to synthesize that and use it in their papers." In contrast,

"I might read that article 100 times and every time I read it, I wasn't really certain of what it was," so "I would use colored highlighters and draw diagrams."

"I was engaging in heroic effort, but not getting very far," she lamented. Worse, "when I looked down the road to my future, actually, I did not see a future—it was bleak and very dark."

Arrowsmith-Young had attempted suicide when she was 13. By the time she was in graduate school, she was again at the end of her tether and decided to attempt suicide again.

She decided to throw herself off the subway platform in Toronto in front of an oncoming train. But before she could commit suicide, fate intervened in the form of a book she discovered by the great pioneering Russian neuroscientist Alexander Luria entitled *The Man with a Shattered World*.

> **Adjustment meant compensating for one's weaknesses by emphasizing one's strengths.**

In the book, Luria discusses the brain injury of a Russian soldier and the effects it had on the soldier's life. "I started to read it and it was the first time that I actually understood what my problem was," says Barbara. "The difficulties he had as a result of a brain wound were the same difficulties I had, and this was a huge 'aha' moment where I started to understand myself."

There was something wrong with her brain and it was causing her to have a learning disability. But her professors did not believe her, which was not surprising.

Remembering the learning trials of her childhood in Canada, she writes: "Almost universally assumed at the time was the idea that you had to play the hand you were dealt because the brain you were born with was fixed and hardwired. Period.

A certain prevailing fatalism meant that I was told I had best learn to adjust."[18]

Adjustment meant compensating for one's weaknesses by emphasizing one's strengths. So, for example, a person who has a problem processing speech based on what that person hears could "hear a sentence but mishear every third or fourth word" or take notes in a classroom but "mishear some words and later discover that your notes make no sense." To compensate for this brain-hearing-processing problem, a person with normal visual abilities could try to read the lips of the speaker to make sense of the spoken words.[19]

Such compensating strategies, which are used in conventional schooling, ignore the fact that science has revealed that the brain is not a fixed unchangeable organ. Rather, as she observes:

> We now take it as given that the brain is inherently plastic, capable of change and constantly changing. The human brain can remap itself, grow new neural connections, and even grow new neurons over the course of a lifetime.[20]

"Neuroplasticity—or brain plasticity—is the ability of the brain to modify its connections or re-wire itself," explains British biomedical scientist Duncan Banks. "Without this ability," he says, "any brain, not just the human brain, would be unable to develop from infancy through to adulthood or recover from brain injury."[21]

Banks says, "Part of the body's ability to recover following damage to the brain can be explained by the damaged area of the brain getting better, but most is the result of neuroplasticity—forming neural connections." To enhance the formation of these neural connections he says:

> As in the developing infant, the key to developing new connections is environmental enrichment that relies on sensory (visual,

auditory, tactile, smell) and motor stimuli. The more sensory and motor stimulation a person receives, the more likely they will be to recover from brain trauma.[22]

The learning dysfunctions from which Arrowsmith-Young suffered caused her to catch only fragments of conversations, never grasping the whole. She could make no sense of the relationship between the big and little hands of a clock. She could not comprehend the logic of basic math, nor could she understand what she was hearing or reading. She had a hard time learning to tie her shoelaces and to distinguish her right hand from her left hand. She was also accident-prone.

> **The learning dysfunctions from which Arrowsmith-Young suffered caused her to catch only fragments of conversations, never grasping the whole.**

Based upon the work of Luria and Mark Rosenzweig, a psychologist at the University of California at Berkeley, Arrowsmith-Young created exercises to change her own brain. Since she could not tell time on a clock, she decided to create a clock-reading exercise using flash cards in order to stimulate that part of her brain.

She believed that she needed to strengthen her brain processing relationships, so she chose clocks because they involve a spatial relationship between the two hands, which are used to tell time.

"I drew 100 different clock faces," she explained, "and I started to shuffle [the cards with the clock faces] and make myself read them."

Over time the exercise worked, and not only could she tell time, she could understand dialogue on television, do math, and even understand jokes.

"I could listen to a conversation," she recalled, "and I could say something back that was appropriate."

Like a blind person whose sight had been miraculously restored, she marveled at what she could now do:

> I had never been able to understand philosophy because it's very conceptual, very abstract. I thought, okay, I'm going to pull a philosophy book off the library shelf and I read a page and got really excited. I actually understood it as I was reading it. Then I pulled another book off the shelf and by the time I was finished, I think I had 100 books stacked all around me. And I had been able to understand each page that I had read.

The change, she said, "was profound and it was clear that there was human neural plasticity because I could now do things that for 26 years, I had never been able to do." "Something fundamentally had changed in my brain."

She then set about to create a program of exercises:

> To change the brain, a program of cognitive treatment needs to deploy what neuroscientists call "activity-dependent neuroplasticity." In 1978 I was using my own intuitive understanding to incorporate this concept into the cognitive exercises I was developing. Simply put, activity-dependent neuroplasticity means that external stimulation that places a demand on the brain over a sustained period of time results in a change to the brain. Based on Rosenzweig's research, I took this concept one step further:

the activity or exercise has to directly target and stimulate the area being addressed. To enhance the focused stimulation, students are instructed not to call on the support of other, perhaps stronger cognitive areas, which would divert stimulation from the area in question. And attention to the prescribed task must be sustained over a period of time to adequately stimulate the intended part of the brain.[23]

It was important to calibrate the exercise to the person's level of functioning. "If the exercise is too hard or too easy," she said, "the brain cannot effectively engage with the task." Thus, she developed multiple levels for each exercise:

Accuracy, automaticity, and consistency of performance are all essential. If you take 30 minutes to do a task that should take 1 minute or if you can accomplish the task only on a hit-or-miss basis, you are not proficient. For each cognitive exercise, we have determined what constitutes proficient performance. Once a student is proficient, he or she moves on to a more difficult level, one that drives effortful processing again.[24]

She says that creating the exercises and watching the change in individuals was like conducting naturalistic experiments: "I learned more and more about each brain area as it improved. As various cognitive functions came online, I saw their workings more clearly."[25]

Over time, she came to understand what happens to the ability to learn when an area of the brain is compromised, and since "each area of the brain is responsible for a different kind of learning, the impact of a deficit in each area of the brain is also different."[26]

The Arrowsmith Program that she developed identifies 19 specific learning dysfunctions. According to University of British Columbia researchers, the program "targets multiple cognitive processing weaknesses, with each student receiving an intervention plan comprised of multiple exercises, each focusing on a different process or combination of processes." The cognitive exercises include:

- motor symbol sequencing, which involves pen-and-paper and complex motor planning;
- symbol relations, which is a computer-based exercise involving conceptual relationships represented on an analogue clock;
- memory for information or instructions, an auditory exercise that involves unrelated information;
- predicative speech, another auditory exercise that involves sequential auditory information;
- Broca's speech pronunciation, which involves speech sound manipulations;
- auditory speech discrimination, which involves speech sounds in an unfamiliar language;
- symbolic thinking, a pen-and-paper exercise that involves language-based material;
- symbol recognition, a computer-based task involving symbolic meaning and memory;
- lexical memory, an auditory word memory exercise;
- kinaesthetic perception, involving drawing or writing with one's eyes closed;
- quantification sense, a computer-based exercise that requires continuous mental calculation;
- nonverbal thinking, a pen-and-paper exercise requiring interpretations of scenarios in pictures;

- object recognition, a computer-based exercise involving object sequences; and

- spatial reasoning, a pen-and-paper exercise involving following pathways within a spatial configuration.[27]

These exercises, write the researchers, "correspond to the 19 areas of learning dysfunction, also developed by Arrowsmith-Young."[28]

In 1980, she established the Arrowsmith School in Toronto, Canada. In 1997, the Toronto Catholic District School Board approved the Arrowsmith Program for Catholic schools across the city. Starting in 2002, several independent schools in Ontario and British Columbia began to offer the Arrowsmith Program. In 2008, the Learning Disabilities Association of Saskatchewan became the first such association in Canada to offer the Arrowsmith Program, which it did at its center in Saskatoon.[29]

Eventually, the Arrowsmith Program spread to other countries. The first Arrowsmith site in the United States opened in 2005, and there are various sites in different states. The program is also available in countries such as Australia, New Zealand, the Cayman Islands, Malaysia, South Korea, Spain, Switzerland, and Thailand.[30]

A key aspect of the Arrowsmith Program, according to the UBC researchers, is that Arrowsmith is longer and more intensive than other interventions, with the typical Arrowsmith student attending the program for 40 weeks over three to four years, completing 200 sessions each year, while other interventions have half the number of sessions.[31]

She observed, "once brain function has been augmented, that gain is permanent." She has tracked her alumni "thirty years removed from the Arrowsmith Program, and there is no loss of function. The changed brain stays changed."[32] The research evidence on the Arrowsmith Program supports her observations.

The 2019 UBC study, published in the peer-reviewed journal *Learning: Research and Practice,* found that the Arrowsmith Program produced "overall academic skill improvement across participants" for those students tracked in the study and concluded that there was "promise for the potential growth children and youth may experience as a result of participation in the Arrowsmith programme."[33]

Other studies have come to similar positive conclusions.

A 2014 University of Calgary study of Arrowsmith's impact on student academic performance found that students with specific learning disabilities who went through the Arrowsmith Program improved their test scores in most academic areas. The study concluded: "Strengthening cognitive/neuropsychological functions presumed to underlie academic achievement deficits improves reading, mathematics, and writing by targeting the cause (i.e., cognitive deficit) rather than the symptoms (i.e., achievement deficit)."[34]

> A key aspect of the Arrowsmith Program, according to the UBC researchers, is that Arrowsmith is longer and more intensive than other interventions.

Further, "Targeted interventions based on knowledge of brain plasticity can lead to improved short-term academic performance across a broad range of domains."[35]

Another University of Calgary study, authored by a different group of researchers, looked at the impact of the Arrowsmith Program on brain weaknesses and cognitive problems. Noting that Arrowsmith "is designed to strengthen cognitive functions underlying specific learning disabilities rather than providing achievement intervention or compensatory strategies," the researchers collected data on students in the Arrowsmith Program and found:

- Children with baseline cognitive difficulties showed significant improvement across cognitive domains in short-term memory, auditory processing, fluid reasoning, and processing speed.

- Given that these cognitive domains are associated with processing weaknesses that underlie most [specific learning disabilities], improvement should ameliorate achievement deficits in children with [specific learning disabilities].

- Results suggest that targeted and individualized interventions designed to remediate cognitive deficits may lead to improved academic performance across a broad range of domains.

- Brain plasticity allows for restructuring of cognitive processes, thereby enabling improved cognition and academic performance.[36]

Other studies by the University of British Columbia, Southern Illinois University, and others also found that the Arrowsmith Program improved a variety of cognitive abilities.[37]

Dr. Greg Rose, who has studied the Arrowsmith program, said that, when studying the program's shorter six-week intensive program, "we actually saw that there were improvements across many areas," based on the Woodcock-Johnson tests of cognitive ability.

He observed that just doing one of the Arrowsmith exercises changes brain networks so that "it is possible that just looking at a clock face all day is helping your ability to count backwards by seven or helping you to write sentences better."

Although more scientific research on Arrowsmith needs to be done, he concluded, "the program has real potential and there's an incredibly strong probability that it produces meaningful results." He is continuing to conduct research on the Arrowsmith program.

"My vision," Arrowsmith-Young has written, "is of a world in which no child ever struggles with a learning disability, no child is ever stigmatized as having one, and no child experiences the ongoing emotional pain of living with a disability." Therefore, "my goal is that every child be assessed at an early age, their brain deficits (major or minor) clearly determined, and tailor-made exercises applied to overcome any learning problems."

Barbara's vision made Mia's journey possible.

CHAPTER SIX
Homeschooling and Training My Brain
Mia Giordano

When my mom found out that I was not going to be allowed to return to Phillips Brooks for my fourth-grade year, she started looking for alternatives. She looked at one private school that specialized in students with learning disabilities, but the strategies they used were compensatory and my core problems would still not be addressed.

In the end, my mom decided on homeschooling as the best option. She proceeded to pull me out of school in February of my third-grade year. I remember I had a Valentine's Day sleepover party for my friends from class and announced that I was leaving school. This announcement was met with a huge "Boo!" and tears.

My mom used the Internet to find great homeschooling resources, and designed a curriculum, which would eventually prove successful for me. She recalls:

It just proved to me over and over again that these in-the-box schools, public and private, don't understand that you can teach kids with multiple issues. You as a parent need to understand that you can do it yourself. Many parents came to me later and asked how I did it because they were afraid. I said there's nothing to be afraid of. It boils down to having confidence in yourself and you have so many opportunities.

Homeschooling is really a great, freeing experience. And the great thing about homeschooling is that if something is not working you can change it.

It was only a month after I was pulled out of Phillips Brooks, in March 2011, that my education psychologist Claire Goss invited my mom to attend a presentation by a man named Howard Eaton, who was going to speak on the Arrowsmith program.

It was a dark and stormy night, just like how Snoopy would always start his novel, and a group of educators, education psychologists, parents and children gathered at a private home to hear Mr. Eaton.

He explained how the Arrowsmith program focused on training the brains of students with learning disabilities so that the weak parts of their brains would be strengthened. He described the exercises that would accomplish this strengthening and eliminate the disabilities. He showed functional MRIs to support his points.

Mr. Eaton ran an Arrowsmith school in Vancouver, Canada. He had written a book, which my mom bought that night. After his presentation, my mom talked to him about me and she soon made arrangements for us to visit the school.

My mom and I flew up to Vancouver, and the school gave me some initial tests and it was determined that I was a perfect candidate for the Arrowsmith program.

My mom was set to enroll me in the Vancouver Arrowsmith school. However, she found out that a small school/learning center in the Bay Area was going to add the Arrowsmith program to the services it offered. Eventually it was decided that I would start there in the fall.

In May 2011, Arrowsmith in California tested me more comprehensively. This assessment tested me for a broad range of cognitive functions in 16 areas. Cognitive functioning is generally defined as mental abilities that include learning, thinking, reasoning, remembering, problem solving, decision-making, and attention.[38] The assessment found specific reasons why I was experiencing my various brain-related problems.

> **He explained how the Arrowsmith program focused on training the brains of students with learning disabilities so that the weak parts of their brains would be strengthened.**

Arrowsmith has a 12-level cognitive-function rating system. The ratings go from very severe at one end to above average at the other end.

Mia had a very severe rating in what is called motor symbol sequencing, which involves producing a symbolic sequential motor pattern such as writing out the alphabet. The processes involve information going through the eye, like reading; then that information going through the hand, like writing; or the information then going through the mouth, like speaking. Arrowsmith says that weakness in this area causes a whole group of problems:

> Misreading – Words are misread due to poorly developed patterns of eye fixations. The person reads "step hall" for a road sign that says "steep hill".

> Handwriting is messy and irregular. People with this dysfunction frequently print rather than handwrite.

> Writing is not automatic. The person has to concentrate on the process of writing and as a result has less attention to focus on the content of what is being written. This also slows down the speed of writing so written assignments and tests often take longer to complete than the allotted time.

> Copying material from one location to another (i.e., from the blackboard or a text into a notebook) is slow and often inaccurate.

> Clerical work is painful and tedious and the person may have a tendency to put it off.

> Spelling – The person can spell the same word several different ways on the same page.

> Speech – The person tends to ramble and have difficulty getting to the point. There is a tendency to leave out chunks of information which are necessary for the

listener to understand what the person is talking about. The person has this information in his head and thinks they have said it but it does not get expressed in speech. It is difficult to get ideas out in the order of their importance in speech, and the person may go back and forth over several subjects, making his speech difficult for others to follow.

Mathematics – This problem affects accuracy in mathematical computations. The person makes what appears to be careless errors but which are really motor slips. For example, the person thinks one number in his head and writes down another number.[39]

Another area where Mia received a severe rating was in symbol relations, which involve connecting concepts and ideas and understanding logical and conceptual relationships. For example, it would be hard to read a clock and understand the relationship between the hands. You can mix up which hand is the hour hand, and which one is the minute hand. You can also misread what the hands are pointing to.[40]

She also had a severe/moderate rating in memory for information and instructions. According to Arrowsmith, "The person has trouble remembering and therefore following lectures or extended conversations or instructions. Instructions often have to be repeated several times before the person is certain of what they are supposed to do, and this certainty doesn't last."[41]

Mia had a severe/moderate rating in something called artifactual thinking, which involves thinking, planning, and problem solving in non-verbal situations. For example, body language and facial expressions would be difficult to interpret.[42]

And she had a moderate/severe problem in symbolic thinking, which involves thinking and problem solving in language-based activities. Among the symptoms for this problem is the inability to keep your attention focused on language-related activity until completion. A person is easily distracted from the activity and may be labeled with an attention problem.[43]

Mia had problems in other areas, but those were the most significant.

So, in the fall of 2011, I started on my new learning journey, which would eventually last for four years. In the mornings I would go to the learning center to receive Arrowsmith instruction. In the afternoons I would go back home to do my academic subjects. I also played tennis because it helped me with my hand and eye coordination.

As I said before, I felt like things were traveling in slow motion, with information traveling more slowly into my brain. In Barbara Arrowsmith's book she mentions a soldier who said that his brain injury caused him to feel like he was in a fog all the time. This perfectly describes how I felt, like there was cotton candy in my brain.

The great thing about Arrowsmith is that the program and the exercises are geared to the individual person and his or her particular brain weakness. So, I received my own individual lesson plan based on what my weaknesses were.

For my motor symbol sequencing problem, because it has to do with eye-hand coordination, I had to do tracing exercises. Initially, there were worksheets with giant green symbols. I had a red pen and I had to trace over the green symbols and not go beyond the border of the symbols. Since I had very messy handwriting and could not stay within the lines on normal writing paper, it was difficult for me to stay within the borders of those symbols. As time went on and I got better at tracing through practice, the width of the symbols would get thinner and thinner ramping up the difficulty.

All the exercises had 13 levels of difficulty. As I mastered one level of difficulty of an exercise, I progressed to the next level.

For symbol relations, I had to do the clocks exercise. People may ask what reading a clock has to do with connecting concepts and relationships between concepts. Howard Eaton, the man my mom heard speak on Arrowsmith, explains:

> I now realize that reading a clock face is an important indicator of a child's ability to understand multiple concepts and to improve

reasoning abilities. A concept is a general idea derived or inferred from specific instances or occurrences. The clock face is quite abstract and requires many concepts to be understood (such as a 24-hour day, 60 minutes in an hour, 60 seconds in a minute and the knowledge that the hands of a clock face signify a placement in time that is constantly moving forward). Of course, there are other concepts, such as before and after, that need to be understood when reading a clock. What is critical for the child is that these concepts need to converge into the ability to look at a clock and tell the time. If the child is struggling to analyze the relationships of all these concepts, it often means they will also struggle with reading comprehension and math problem solving, as these achievement abilities also require the ability to analyze and synthesize many concepts simultaneously.[44]

These clock exercises did not just involve reading a clock with only a minute hand and an hour hand. As the exercises got more difficult, the number of hands on the clock would increase. Eventually, the clock could have up to 10 hands. Each hand represents a particular place in time, from seconds to centuries. Deciphering the clock with speed and accuracy helped my reasoning abilities, my reading comprehension and my math problem solving.

For my problems with retaining information and following instructions, I had to do an exercise called Phrases. Due to my auditory processing issues, I had to listen to a complete phrase and repeat it back. The phrase would not be a normal phrase, such as "the chicken crossed the road." Instead, the phrase could be more abstract such as "chicken road crossed into tree." You had to then repeat that phrase back three times in a row perfectly. The phrases would get longer and harder.

I started doing the phrases exercise in my third year in Arrowsmith and found it to be really, really difficult.

To address my problems in symbolic thinking, I had to do an exercise called L-Think. In this exercise I was given a small passage to read and then I would have to say verbally what was the main idea of the passage. I would also have to write down the main idea because different areas of the brain control your verbal and writing abilities.

For my artifactual thinking problems, I had to do an exercise called R-Think, which involved looking at a picture, like a Norman Rockwell painting, and then writing down a detailed description of what was going on in the picture. I had to look at the whole picture and explain why things were happening in the picture, not just details I could see in the picture. I had to interpret facial expressions and body language, plus interpret meaning from the context of the picture. I would first start to do this exercise in my third year in Arrowsmith.

Another exercise I had to do was symbol recognition. I would be shown a symbol on a computer screen. I would look at that symbol for as long as I wanted to look at it and try to brand that symbol in my memory. Then, I would click for the next computer screen, which would have dozens of symbols on the screen. I would then have to find the original symbol that had been given to me. As the difficulty level got harder, I was given multiple symbols to remember and subsequently identify.

Also, I placed an eye patch over my left eye and repeatedly wrote a particular symbol or set of symbols on paper for an hour.

These symbol recognition exercises were designed to help me with things such as taking notes when teachers would write on a board.

I would spend half the day doing Arrowsmith exercises at the learning center. Also, I would alternate exercises depending on the day.

Looking back on my nine-year-old self, what did I think about Arrowsmith? I remember the repetitiveness. I know the exercises were based on repeating things in order to strengthen the weak parts of my brain. However, for a nine-year-old to do those exercises day after day was boring. So boring.

I also had to do Arrowsmith homework, like my tracing exercises, and that was extremely boring, too.

Because I thought the program was boring, I started to slack off and not try as hard. My mom saw that I was not focusing like I should have been, but instead of nagging me she decided I needed to learn a lesson about effort and results. Although she explained to me what I needed to do in order to improve my brain functions, she basically put me in charge of my own success.

Well, of course, I did not make the progress that I should have been making. In a meeting with my Arrowsmith teacher Kelly Ferreira, who I really loved, she pointed out how I was not making advances. It was at that moment that it hit me that I really needed to try hard and focus on training my brain so I would not suffer from the issues that had plagued me during my life. I remember looking up at my mom and telling her, "You're right."

I really was in charge of my own destiny. So, I told myself that I had to really focus on doing well on my Arrowsmith exercises.

Focus and persistence would be critical for my success. Arrowsmith is not like the 100-yard dash. As a multi-year program, it is much more like the marathon. I would have to be committed for the long haul and now I was.

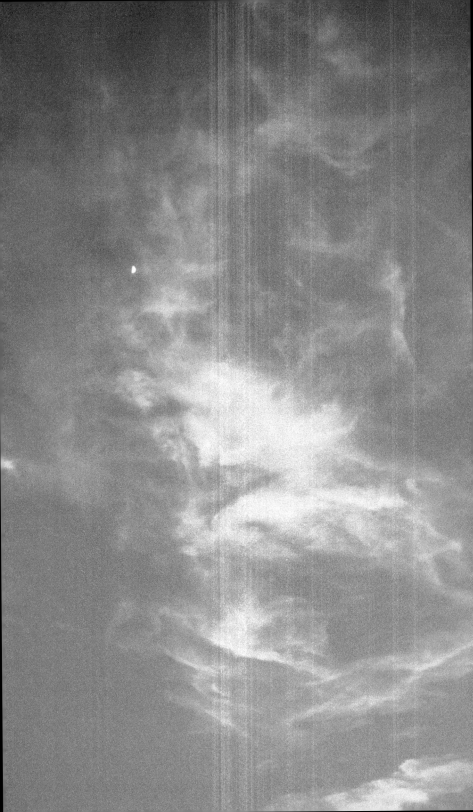

CHAPTER SEVEN
How a Teacher Changed Her Mind
Lance Izumi

Speaking of Mia, Kelly Ferreira says, "She's really a re-markable young woman."

Kelly should know because she was Mia's Arrowsmith teacher for four years and saw firsthand how the Arrowsmith program allowed Mia "the freedom to grow and to blossom."

Born in the Flint, Michigan area, where generations of her ancestors lived and farmed, Ferreira recalls, "I was always the math-science nerd." When her classmates skipped out on science classes when they had to perform dissections, she would tell them, "go ahead, I'll cover for you, and I'll dissect yours."

So, when it came time for her to go to college, she headed down Interstate 75 from Michigan to Florida and studied nursing, with an emphasis on pediatric neurology.

"I found the brain to be so fascinating," she said, and "the first surgery I saw in school was brain surgery." The surgery was primitive compared to today, but from that moment she remembered, "I just fell in love with the brain, so I started studying it immediately."

After she got married, she moved to California. She had two daughters and noticed that even when they were little, she could see a difference in one of them and how she communicated and took in information. "Her receptive and expressive language skills were very, very high," she said, "yet, there were other pieces of her development that were not on track." Eventually, "as I did discover, that they had some learning differences."

Her daughter had dyslexia, which is a learning disorder that causes those with the condition to have difficulty in reading due to their problems in identifying speech sounds and learning how those sounds relate to letters and words.[45] Every year, around three million individuals are diagnosed with dyslexia.

Because of her interests during her nursing studies and her daughter's dyslexia, she had a great deal of both academic and practical training in learning disabilities.

"I ended up with this passion for kids with learning disabilities," she explained, "and I am just passionate about making a difference in our country and how we address the abilities of different students."

She eventually enrolled her daughter in the Charles Armstrong private school in Belmont, outside of San Francisco. The school specializes in teaching children with language-based learning problems, such as dyslexia. She ended up working at the school.

Eventually, she left Charles Armstrong to work on some private research projects and was contacted by a former colleague who asked her if she had ever heard of Barbara Arrowsmith-Young and the Arrowsmith program based in Canada. Kelly had not, but warned her acquaintance "with all due respect, everybody's got a silver bullet out there that they're trying to sell that is the answer to everyone's learning disabilities, and I've come to believe that there isn't a silver bullet."

Her friend, she recalled, forthrightly responded, "I'm not asking your opinion of it, I want to hire you to do some research and find out if it's worth bringing to the Bay Area."

Still the skeptic, Ferreira, who has relatives in Canada, said, "Well, you are going to pay me to go visit my family, pretty much like a paid vacation, and I'm probably going to come home with the same story that I didn't find a silver bullet." Her former colleague said it would still be worth it because she wanted to do whatever she could to help children in need, including her own children who had learning difficulties.

In her research on the Arrowsmith program, she found out, that the program "is neuro-cognitive therapy." "Barbara Arrowsmith-Young," she discovered, "has isolated several areas of the brain that support learning and communication in their own specific way," and she has "developed exercises that will strengthen neural pathways that carry the information to and from different areas of the brain."

Today, she uses the following example to explain the Arrowsmith program:

> When I talk to parents, especially, and to educators, I ask them if they remember the diagnosis of lazy eye, and most people will say that they remember. And then I will ask them what the treatment was for it. And they said a person would wear an eye patch and the patch be placed on the good eye. And I said that's exactly the premise of these neurocognitive exercises—force the weak area of the brain to do the work. Take away the support of the strong eye or any other stronger areas of the brain so it strengthens the weak area. What's different about the brain is that once the weak area of the brain is strengthened, you don't lose it, unless you have a brain injury.

She went to Canada and started interviewing people who had gone through the Arrowsmith program and were then currently in the program. Most of the people would tell her similar stories.

"They came out of desperation and personal failure," she said, "whether as children or as adults." And the universal positive outcomes that they experienced caused them to say the same thing: "Everybody I talked to, including high school students, postgraduate students, and adults said if they could have done this before junior high their lives could have been so much different."

In fact, when she asked these people how the program was working for them, "Most people gave me this message: the Arrowsmith program changed my life." Specifically, these individuals told her:

> It wasn't easy, it's not a walk on the beach, but it is a game changer. They were desperate and needed the game changed. And so, it may not have been the most fun they ever had, but it was the most productive thing they ever did. They told me over and over again, I wish I would have done it sooner. I even asked adults who did it years and decades ago, and married with their own children, would you put your children in this program if it was necessary, and they said in a heartbeat.

One of the interesting things she discovered was that Canada has a form of school choice. According to a report by the Heritage Foundation:

> A unique constitutional "wrinkle" exists in the Canadian context as a result of pre-Confederation (pre-1867) negotiations to preserve approaches to education that were themselves the result of the unique attempt to pre-

serve the rights of parents to educate children in their own religion, culture, and language. Expressed in constitutional terms, the right of the Protestant or Roman Catholic minority in each province to its own, separate education system was preserved. The end result of Canada's unique constitutional framework is that experiments in school choice have not only been preserved but expanded, as choice between at least two systems has always been a feature of many Canadian provinces.[46]

In the case, for example, in the province of Alberta, school choice has been an important part of the province's education history:

Historically, the province of Alberta has had two taxpayer-funded school systems. The first is the secular "public" system, while the second is the "separate" system, which on occasion can be aligned with a denomination. (For example, in Alberta's largest city, Calgary, the fully funded separate school system is officially known as the Calgary Catholic School District). The latter is partly the result of historical settlement in the province; it is also the result of Canada's linguistic and cultural duality in which English and French language rights have constitutional protection, and education rights flow from the same.

The presence of this second, separate, school system, fully funded by the province of Alberta, had led to competition and choice. In Alberta, those who pay property taxes can and do choose which system to fund when asked by civic census takers.[47]

Ferreira found that in Canada, "your school taxes, you can decide where they go," and that the Arrowsmith program had been adopted by the Catholic school system in Toronto: "It's just part of the woodwork when kids enrolled in school." Thus, the Catholic schools "integrate [Arrowsmith] exercises in their school day" for children who have non-autism-related learning problems.

She explains that where Arrowsmith is part of a seven-period school day, children who need Arrowsmith may do the exercises in zero period. These children would then go to their math period, then their English period and so forth, "and then they come back into the Arrowsmith classroom and do [exercises]." "And that is the optimal way to do it," she says.

She found, however, in areas where students "missed most of fourth or fifth or sixth grade doing the Arrowsmith program," they came back and did an intensive summer program in the basic subjects "and they not only went in at their next grade, but they just excelled."

Ferreira made it clear that she only talked to those who participated in the Arrowsmith program and purposely did not talk to anyone from the Arrowsmith program itself. She wanted to do an independent evaluation.

In the end, she said, "I was sold, I was completely sold." In fact, she was so "sold" that she eventually became an Arrowsmith teacher in the San Francisco Bay Area. It was then that she met Mia.

Mia and her mother Christine had gone to an Arrowsmith informational meeting in the Bay Area that featured Howard Eaton, who pioneered Arrowsmith in Canadian education. Ferreira recalled:

> Christine and Mia came to one of the [informational] sessions and I have to tell you, I was drawn to them immediately. Mia is so stinking adorable, is so entertaining, and so engaging. And we chatted away, and I said Mia is the perfect typical candidate for the program.

Why was Mia the perfect candidate for Arrowsmith? Because, said Ferreira:

> She is average to above average in IQ. She does not have behavior disorders. She is not on the [autism] spectrum. She is motivated; she wanted to learn; she wanted to make a difference; and she was able to wrap her head around [the program] . . . . You've got to have buy-in with students for them to do this. But not every student could [handle] this type of work. Mia, on the other hand, was well aware of what she struggled in. She had a wonderful perspective and outlook, and she was positive. And she knew she could do it. That's not to say it was a little glide across the pond for her. It was a challenge. There were days that she cried and days that I cried, and days that we gave each other tissues. It was hard.

Yet, despite the trials and difficulties, Mia succeeded. But why did she succeed? Because, said Ferreira, in addition to all of her great qualities, the Arrowsmith tutoring center that Mia attended while she was being homeschooled "was not a conventional school," but "was a center for students with learning and language issues, speech and language issues, developmental delays, and it was not a typical school." In other words, it was an educational choice option that did not use the dominant paradigm in the conventional schools.

Mia had a variety of learning issues. According to Ferreira, Mia's "ability to read and comprehend was grossly delayed. "She couldn't read, she couldn't write," and her "math was horrible."

Especially significant, however, was Mia's difficulty in the area of executive function. Kelly explained:

Executive function in a classroom is the kid who can't take the initiative to get started because they have no idea really where they're at. They're the ones that could even do homework at school, but it never makes it into the classroom to get turned in the next day or even that same day. They're the ones that have the things wadded in the bottom of their backpack and six weeks later emerges with a smashed banana on it.

In Mia's case, Ferreira said that Mia had difficulty with social cues, such as "what's happening now in this room, what happened before this, and what might happen afterwards." Thus, "Without her mom, I couldn't imagine her getting through the day."

One of the ways that the Arrowsmith program diagnoses executive-function issues, involved, of all things, Norman Rockwell pictures:

One of the things that we use for executive function and social skills and learning to read facial expression and body language is we actually use work from Norman Rockwell. And these wonderful Americana, pictures he painted throughout the decades, we would use those and have students tell a story of what's going on with that. And Mia was completely lost. She is so articulate and so creative, she could make up a story that has zero to do with the picture she was looking at. So, there is a process of bringing them back to take a look at the picture and asking, "What do you think they're feeling? What do you think happened before that caused them to feel that way? What do you think they're going to do?" . . . But that was pretty remarkable using those [pictures]. She would come up with hilarious one-liners, because one of the things I would ask is what is the main idea . . . of this picture. She was pretty entertaining as she would try to do that.

So how did the Arrowsmith program address Mia's executive function deficiencies? Ferreira said, "what we did for the executive function was really quite simple and quite beautiful."

The Arrowsmith program, she said, evaluates different areas of the brain, and for each of the weak areas, there are exercises. One of the exercises Mia was asked to do involved clocks.

The exercise started by focusing on the hands of the clock. The important concept is to understand that when one hand of the clock moves, the other moves in synchronization. "And it's the incremental moves, that when this hand goes this far, the other hand goes this far," noted Ferreira.

Mia would be given exercises with clocks on paper and drawing and redrawing the hands. Ferreira explained: "Drawing the exact time of the hour and the minute, and then we add the second hand and then the 60th of a second. Then we add the day the month, the year, and the decade."

One might ask how drawing hands on a clock could be connected to improving executive functions and reasoning. It turns out that there is a brain connection.

In Barbara Arrowsmith-Young's groundbreaking book *The Woman Who Changed Her Brain*, she recalled a very young boy named Zachary who had problems in the symbol-relations are of the brain, which is the juncture of the parietal-temporal-occipital regions of the brain. This part of the brain "integrates and attaches meaning to information from sensory modalities in order to understand the world." Thus, "The part of Zachary's brain necessary for processing information coming from those senses and attaching meaning to it was not working properly."[48]

Zachary, who hated school, "would completely and utterly freeze and stop listening to any instructions because he knew he couldn't understand them." In other words, "He had no ability to reason."[49]

To address his issues, his mother enrolled him in the Arrowsmith program, which started him on clock exercises. Initially, he could not understand the connection between the big hand and the little hand. In order to help him, he was asked to pretend he was one of the hands of the clock:

> To help Zachary understand the movement of the hands of a clock, Chris [the Arrowsmith teacher] told him to get up and hold her hand. "Pretend you're the hour hand and I'm the minute hand," she said. "I'm taller than you, so the minute hand is longer than the hour hand. I said, 'Now I'm walking. What are you doing?' He says, 'I'm walking.' I said, 'Okay, but are you walking beside me or are you following me?' He says, 'I'm following you.' I said, 'That's what happens with the hour hand. The minute hand moves and the hour hand moves more slowly behind it.'" Zachary's deficit was so severe that he could not understand the abstract concept of how the two hands move together until he physically experienced it himself.[50]

Six months into the Arrowsmith program, things began to change for him. At the start of the program the part of his brain necessary for making connections was so impaired that it was as if he lived inside a box. Yet, after repeatedly doing the Arrowsmith exercises, "He was stepping out of that box," becoming more social, and "was starting to reason, to lose some of the anxiety, and to feel good about himself."[51] Further:

> "Zachary's comprehension improved," says Chris, the Arrowsmith teacher, "because he got things the first time. There were times in the beginning of the school year where you'd

have to explain to him how to do one of the exercises five different ways, and he would still ask the same question because he just didn't understand what you were saying." No longer.

Because Zachary's world had been so confusing, and he could not attach reasons to behavior, he could not explain why he did not want to do an activity. He would shut down and give this standard response: "I don't want to do this. It's stupid." What may have looked like a behavior problem was not. "And as this cognitive area improved," Chris says, "he was able to verbalize why he was doing something or why he was feeling the way he was without me cueing him in any way."[52]

Zachary's mother saw a slow transformation in her son as the cognitive exercises strengthened the weaker part of his brain and allowed her son to engage with the outside world. "The biggest change for me," she said, "was that he communicated and had relationships with people other than me. I had been carrying the burden of being his sole communicator."[53]

Chris, the Arrowsmith teacher, said that at the beginning of his time in the program, Zachary was extremely miserable. Eventually, however, he became "a shining star. Everyone in the class adored him."[54]

Mia's experience was similar to Zachary's. Like Zachary, Mia had big challenges at the start of the Arrowsmith program. Showing up every day and doing the same exercises may seem monotonous to a child, observed Ferreira, "but don't forget, we're working on the weakest part of their brain, and that's where the tears were from—like I'm never going to get any better."

The challenge was keeping the students motivated, she said, "looking at it like a journey and this is one more step." Sometimes, "it felt like we were climbing Everest without oxygen, and other times we felt like we just reached the summit." But reaching one summit also meant there was another to climb.

Yet, like Zachary, Mia started to make progress. Constantly doing the various Arrowsmith exercises was strengthening the weak part of her brain and her executive-function skills gradually started to improve.

One could see the improvement, said Ferreira, "in the way Mia interacted with other students, her appropriate responses to students, and her ability not to respond when it was a socially inappropriate situation." "I saw a real shift in her," recalled Kelly.

Indeed, by the end of her time in the Arrowsmith program, Kelly said, "you would never think that [executive function] was an issue with her."

Mia was not just making strides in her social skills, but also in her academic skills. Previously, she had huge problems with reading and writing. But after the effects of the exercises started to take hold, Ferreira said Mia's writing became articulate and "her sentences were able to come together and make sense."

In the Academy Award-winning film "The King's Speech," King George VI, a lifelong stutterer, is able to recite from Shakespeare through the assistance of his speech therapist Lionel Logue. Logue tells the king, "You were sublime." Mia also had a sublime moment.

"I recall," said Ferreira, "one day Mia writing something and she brought it to me, and I asked, 'Man, who wrote this?' And she had tears in her eyes, and I said, 'You wrote this and I can read it.'" "The words were spelled correctly and this kid had not been in a conventional classroom learning all the things she had missed," she explained, but "I could actually read what she wrote, and she spelled phonetically, and it was absolutely beautiful."

Of course, as with Zachary, Mia's improvements were incremental. In the Arrowsmith exercises, there are several levels to go through, and as Ferreira indicated, "in each level, there are several milestones to hit, and so it typically takes three to five years to finish the program, depending on what their issues are." Thus, there are a lot of exercises, a lot of levels, a lot of milestones, and "she can't do them all at once."

So, for example, Mia "couldn't start the clock exercise until she was far enough along in math to add up to 60, as well as skip counting by six and by 12." For Mia and other students, it could be frustrating, but then, notes Kelly, "suddenly something clicks and they take off."

In Mia's case, she eventually became so adept at the clock exercise that Ferreira made her a clock tutor for new students in the program: "I'd say, Mia, help them out. Tell them how it works. Mia did that so beautifully as the clock expert in the classroom. She didn't just sit down with them and say, well, you do this, this and this. She patiently walked through every step of the way. And I would hear my little speeches coming out, and she was 13 years old talking to college students. It was awesome."

In the end, Ferreira says that Mia "is going to be the girl who makes a big change in whatever her passion takes her," and "I feel privileged and humbled and honored to have been a part of it."

CHAPTER EIGHT

Things Start to Improve
Mia Giordano

I t began with small changes.

I could talk more fluently, making whole sentences that actually made sense. My stutter got better and completely stopped by the end of my second year of Arrowsmith. These may seem like small steps to some people, but they were giant strides for me.

My brain previously seemed like it was filled with this jumble of words and information. It would take forever for my brain to decode things and then get it out of me. Now, as I was doing the Arrowsmith exercises, I was able to process all that information in my brain so I could speak.

During my second year in the Arrowsmith program, I did very well in my clocks exercises. I was reading clocks that had the hour, minute, second, and 60th-of-a-second hand. In fact, by the end of my second year I was reading clocks with eight hands on them.

Writing symbols on paper with an eye patch over one of my eyes was difficult. The exercise required me to write the symbols down quickly, which meant that I had to be very focused and not distracted. Although that exercise was difficult, I persevered and eventually started to get better at it.

Tracing was the hardest exercise for me. I had to keep my hand very steady and use this red pen to write within the borders of this green symbol. Trying to get my eyes, brain and hand to cooperate was not easy. But the more I did it the better I got.

I did very well with the L-Think exercises, which had me read little passages and write down the main idea of the passage. I could retain information from the story easier and as a result could read better.

Indeed, my progress in Arrowsmith had an enormous impact on my academic studies, which I was doing in my afternoons. Due to my hard work and determination, when my reading improved and my retention increased, other subjects such as history became easier.

Math, which had always been tough for me, became less of a challenge as well. I could retain information like formulas, memorize procedures, which in turn made arithmetic operations much easier. I felt true triumph when I did not have to use my fingers to add or subtract and I could do division in my head.

The exercises were starting to train the weak parts of my brain, making them stronger. As a result, I was noticing big differences.

For my mom, she was very happy to see me improving. As she said:

> Arrowsmith is grinding work. It's painstaking and tedious. You're exhausted when you are done. And for this little girl to then have to transition after lunch and do her math, science, and language arts was not an easy thing to do. But what was great was that she was more positive and upbeat the second year.

As the one who made the decision about my education, my mom said that she took a leap of faith that Arrowsmith would help me get better. She felt like she was a pioneer and it really opened her eyes to understanding the world of education in so many ways. Too many people in our country are stuck in this one-size-fits-all mindset, and my mom and I want all children to have the opportunities that I had.

As my brain improved, my social world improved as well. I had a lot more friends. The number of students at the Arrowsmith learning center increased from six the first year to around 20 the second year. We now had a community of students there who could help and support each other.

My mom had joined with another homeschooling mom to do homeschooling together, which allowed me to get to know more kids.

I started to develop more interests. I became interested in the outdoors, like climbing on trees. I was able to play better with other kids, including boys. I played in the dirt with the boys and built things with my hands. There were boys everywhere. I enjoyed sports such as swimming, skiing, and especially tennis. In fact, I really started to focus in on tennis. I felt like a normal 10-year-old, which made me feel a lot better about myself.

We joined a homeschooling social group, which brought together homeschool families from the peninsula area south of San Francisco. On Tuesdays, the group would have a family game night where people would bring pizza and board games for parents and kids to play. People who do not know anything about homeschooling always assume that kids do not get to have social lives with other kids. That is a huge myth.

I was homeschooled for years and I made tons of friends through homeschooling. I remember meeting two girls in the homeschooling social group who were from a different city than where I lived. It turned out that we all liked classical music, and we all went to the opera together. The point is, I would never have met these great girls if it were not for homeschooling.

All in all, things were really on the upswing as I entered my third year in the Arrowsmith program.

In my third year, I started to do the R-Think exercise to address my problems with artifactual thinking, which involves thinking, planning, and problem solving in non-verbal situations. This was the exercise where I had to look at a picture and then write down the meaning of the picture based on things like facial expressions, body language, and the context of the picture.

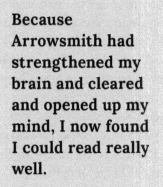

Because Arrowsmith had strengthened my brain and cleared and opened up my mind, I now found I could read really well.

For example, in the famous Norman Rockwell painting of the policeman and the little boy sitting at the counter of a restaurant, you have to notice everything to pick up the narrative and meaning the picture is trying to create and convey to the viewer.

The R-Think exercise was very difficult for me because I started off just seeing little details, but not the deeper meaning of the picture. However, by the end of my third year, I had gotten better and showed major improvement.

I also started doing the exercise on phrases in my third year. As I mentioned earlier, in this exercise a phrase would be said to me and I had to keep that phrase in my mind and say it back to the teacher three times in a row correctly. As I progressed, the phrases would become harder and more abstract.

The reason I had such trouble with the phrases exercise was because of my auditory processing issues. When I heard something, a lot of what I heard seemed to go out the other side of my head. I would retain only parts of what I heard, and it would take me a long time to try and understand those parts that were floating around in my brain and to keep things in my brain.

However, after about two months of doing the phrases exercise, it became a lot easier for me. I could repeat the phrases, which meant that they were sticking in my brain, which was processing the phrases, even when they were abstract and did not make sense.

I continued to do my clocks and tracing exercises.

I made great progress in tracing. Arrowsmith exercises have 13 different difficulty levels. I had been stuck at level seven for a long time, but then something clicked and I zoomed up to level 10, which is where I finished at the end of my third year.

I was improving in the clocks exercise, too. I had finished my second year at level six. By the end of my third year, I was at level eight.

So, overall, I had made major progress from my first to my third year in Arrowsmith. People may ask what evidence was there that Arrowsmith was changing my life. Well, here is one big piece of evidence.

Because Arrowsmith had strengthened my brain, which cleared and opened up my mind, I now found I could read really well. When I had all my brain issues, I disliked reading and it was hard for me to read a handful of books. You can't like what you can't do.

But when my reading skills improved, I fell in love with reading. After the summer of my third year in Arrowsmith I read 53 books—yes, 53!

Reading became fun because I could not only read the words, but I could put them together to understand the story. Now, it was like a light bulb went off in my head and I could see the words forming a story.

The books I started reading became more and more complex. I found so much joy in delving into history books, especially World War II, and historical fiction. Through my reading, I began building my beliefs and philosophy with each book that passed through my hands.

In other words, I started to become this full whole person, not just this little girl limited by her learning disabilities.

CHAPTER NINE

The Education Psychologist and the Impossibility of Changing Conventional School Systems

Lance Izumi

"My belief system changed," says Claire Goss. That is how Mia's case altered the views of the education psychologist who advised her family.

Much of the trajectory of Goss' life was fairly conventional. She majored in psychology as an undergraduate at the State University of New York at Stony Brook, worked as a teacher, and then went on to get a master's degree in school psychology.

She worked in a Connecticut school district, moved to California with her husband, and then worked as a school psychologist for the San Mateo County Office of Education in the San Francisco Bay Area.

Working at a government agency, however, felt professionally confining to her.

"In 2007," she recalled, "I said that's it." "I'm not serving the kids the way I want to serve them." She took an early retirement and then established her own private practice.

"What I wanted to do," said Goss, "was really help kids and families understand that we all learn differently and there are many, many different approaches that could be addressed, but in public education you have boxes you have to fit kids into."

What kind of boxes? Mia provides a perfect example.

If Mia had been in the public schools, Goss said that she would have been given "45 minutes a day of resource help with maybe 10 kids in the same room, maybe an aide supporting in the early grades." The 45-minute sessions would be given four to five days a week.

The time allotted to this focused help would be strictly regulated and the type of help Mia would have received would have been a one-size-fits-all approach with little consideration of outside-the-box alternatives.

So, Mia, who had auditory difficulties, would have received instruction that emphasized those senses that were strong. Goss notes, "If you had an auditory issue, they would emphasize the visual, so it's compensatory."

That compensatory strategy is contrary to the Arrowsmith program's emphasis on strengthening the weak parts of the brain to make them as strong as the rest of the brain.

"The big thing in special education in public education," observes Goss, is "you're not supposed to supplant a program, you're supposed to help with compensatory education to support what's happening in the regular classroom."

What the regular public schools would have provided Mia would not have worked, says Goss, and "I think I would have seen a much more frustrated little girl."

But it is important to understand that the issue is not public versus private schools, but conventional schooling versus unconventional education.

Mia's parents took her out of a public school and placed her in a private school that could not address her difficulties and needs. And even a nearby private school that catered to dyslexic students would not have been a good fit for her.

"So, there aren't a whole lot of options, even in the private sector for kids like Mia," says Goss.

Mia's first appointment with Goss occurred in February 2009 when she was in the first grade. Goss interviewed Mia, spent some time with her, and administered some diagnostic tests.

Goss said that she saw a child with significant auditory difficulties that contributed to memory problems. Further, "she needed help in the area of speech and language" because her auditory and language issues were connected and therefore "she wasn't picking up the sound-symbol relationships."

After that initial meeting, Mia's mother Christine recalled, "The best thing about that first meeting is that when it was over, Claire came to me and said I agree with you, I know there's a medical problem and I can hear it in her breathing."

Goss recommended the doctor who correctly diagnosed Mia's medical problems, including her sleep apnea, which was eventually addressed through surgery.

Having Goss on board also helped in her dealings with Mia's school.

"I had it on record with the school," said Christine, "that I was collaborating with an education psychologist," which was important because schools tend to look at parents "as if you don't know anything." "So, I had to have the muscle behind me with Claire."

Goss made recommendations to Phillips Brooks school about accommodation strategies for Mia. Mia's teachers would contact Goss about questions or changes.

"We came up with the idea of a school within a school," said Goss, "so Mia would have the envelope of Phillips Brooks school, because there were certainly classes that don't require her to have the [added] attention," such as art and physical education.

According to Christine, Mia's second-grade teacher "was 100 percent on board" with the accommodation strategy and there seemed to be progress "to where we thought we could continue with this."

The accommodations for Mia included having a tutor who would work with her on special reading lessons, using the Slingerland approach, which is a structured, sequential, simultaneous, multisensory teaching approach that is designed to help dyslexic students and other struggling readers with speaking, reading, writing, and spelling.[55] As the tutor worked with Mia, the other students in the class would work on the regular reading lessons.

However, when Mia was in the third grade the accommodations for her were not being followed. Her confidence then began to deteriorate.

The third grade is often a pivotal time. Goss notes that in the third grade the subject matter becomes more difficult and more rigorous, and Mia "wasn't ready for that."

"The breakdown," says Goss, "was that the difficulty of the material and speed with which the material was being given was a challenge for Mia, compounded with the fact that the teacher was not giving her the simple instructions that had been enumerated."

Because of the breakdown, embarrassing incidents would occur in class. She would ask the teacher a question and the teacher would repeat the answer that she had given previously. Mia would still not understand and ask the question again. The rest of the children in the class would then give out a collective groan.

While all this sadness was taking place, Christine had been talking to Goss about what she was learning about the brain.

She had read Dr. Norman Doidge's landmark 2007 book *The Brain that Changes Itself.* According to Doidge's website:

> The brain can change itself. It is a plastic, living organ that can actually change its own structure and function, even into old age. Arguably the most important breakthrough in neuroscience since scientists first sketched out the brain's basic anatomy, this revolutionary discovery, called neuroplasticity, promises to overthrow the centuries-old notion that the brain is fixed and unchanging. The brain is not, as was thought, like a machine, or "hardwired" like a computer. Neuroplasticity not only gives hope to those with mental limitations, or what was thought to be incurable brain damage, but expands our understanding of the healthy brain and the resilience of human nature.[56]

Doidge's book was a revelation to Christine, who says, "I was getting frustrated with these teachers and administrators being so finite and definite about ability."

"The backstory," she explains, "is that I already expressed to Claire that there's got to be another, better way because the brain is not static."

While that conversation was going between Christine and Goss, however, the wheels were falling off the cart for Mia at school.

There were insinuations from those associated with the school that Mia was depressed, which were debunked by her physician. Yet, Christine felt that her daughter was being set up.

Indeed, during the fall semester of third grade, the school sent a letter to Mia's family saying that Mia could finish out the year at Phillips Brooks, but would not be offered the opportunity to come back for the fourth grade.

As Goss points out, "Don't think that just because you send a child to a private school that you're going to get more individualized attention and that you're going to get more understanding."

After Christine discussed the letter with Goss, she says, "what we decided was that we're not going to waste Mia's time because it is a waste to keep her . . . in a place where she's not wanted." So, after Valentine's Day in the spring semester, she pulled Mia out of Phillips Brooks in order to homeschool her.

Not long after Christine started homeschooling Mia, Goss received a flyer about a local event featuring a talk by Howard Eaton, who had established the Eaton Arrowsmith School in Vancouver, Canada in 2005.[57]

The Eaton Arrowsmith School uses Barbara Arrowsmith-Young's program to address the needs of students with differences and disabilities. Eaton's school is modeled after the Arrowsmith School in Toronto, which has been operating with great success since 1980.

Goss asked Christine to join her at the event, which they both ended up attending. Christine talked with Eaton after the event. Goss was initially skeptical about the idea of brain change, but she did not dismiss it out of hand.

"I said it was voodoo medicine," she recalls, "because it was so different than any of my training, but it made sense to me, and knowing Christine and her openness, I thought this is perfect."

While listening to Eaton, she says, "I'm thinking, well, from a neurological point of view, the research made sense and it wasn't voodoo medicine."

She also recalled from her days at SUNY Stony Brook working with animals that it is possible to change the neurons, and "this was an approach that was changing the firing of the neurons, which makes sense to me."

Although it was hard for her to wrap her head around the Arrowsmith method, with its exercises involving clocks and tracing, "I could see how this could change things versus a regular reading or math curriculum."

She acknowledges, "even though I'm a psychologist, I don't believe that the tests we use as educational psychologists tell the true picture." More important and more accurate, "I think it's day-to-day performance and actually observing pre and post what Mia could be doing, and if there was a difference I could see it."

After Mia started the Arrowsmith program in the Bay Area and started making progress, Goss remembers going to the Giordano's home and seeing what Mia was doing. She saw the positive change in her writing, motor response, and creative response.

After several years of Arrowsmith, according to Goss, "Mia had made the change that she needed to make in her brain to be successful academically just about anywhere."

Comparing Mia before and after Arrowsmith, Goss said, "her reasoning skills and her auditory processing skills went through the roof." "It was a dramatic change," she concluded.

Like Dr. Anne Weisman, Goss brought up the issue of equity, saying, "not all children would have been able to do this because, number one, they didn't have parents that believed in it and someone had to pay for it."

From a systemic point of view, Arrowsmith would be impossible to implement in regular public school systems. Says Goss, "The only way this would work in the public school system is if we had a complete paradigm shift," but "the structure of the public education system is just not built to handle something like this—teachers aren't trained, the belief system isn't there, and the funding isn't there."

She also points to state education codes that dictate how many hours are to be devoted to various subjects, which would make it difficult to implement a time-intensive program like Arrowsmith. "It doesn't align," she says, "you'd be out of compliance."

However, if Mia was forced to comply with the dictates of the state and its structured paradigm, Goss emphasized, "she would have adhered to what the state and the government wanted her to do, but in the end her life wouldn't be better."

As a public education administrator, Goss says, "What proved to be successful for Mia is virtually impossible in terms of public education." "No way, no how."

Barbara Arrowsmith-Young herself points to the inability of the education status quo to change and consider models outside the accepted paradigms.

"A paradigm shift," she observes, is when some anomalies start to occur that you can't explain in the current paradigm." Most people ignore the anomalies or discount them "because they don't fit into their paradigm."

Arrowsmith-Young gives the shocking example of one noted educator who acknowledged the reality of neuroplasticity, but who still says, "it has no place in education."

She has invited education psychologists to join her research initiatives and to talk to those researching her program, but "they're not interested, they don't engage, they've already made up their mind, they're not open." "They've already decided that this can't be possible."

These establishment educators are "still in the old paradigm where you have to accept our limitations and where learning disabilities are a lifelong condition."

The old paradigm pushed by establishment educators, she says, spells eventual disaster in life for young people with learning disabilities:

> They believe in the fixed mindset, where strength and weaknesses cannot change. So, accept that profile and modify the external to meet that profile. But it's not addressing the problem. You can have all the accommodations in school, but who on the job is going to accommodate or give you a compensation? So, we are not preparing students for the future. And to me, you learn with your brain. If you can strengthen critical aspects of cognitive functions in the brain, you are preparing the student for life.

The inherent inability of the public school system to adapt in order to include successful paradigm-shifting methods such as Arrowsmith is tragic for the countless children whose lives will not be improved. That is why parents must have the opportunity to choose among education options that best meet the needs of their children. Chapter 13 of this book will flush out the importance of educational choice.

CHAPTER TEN

Fourth and Final Year
Mia Giordano

*F*airy tales always conclude with a happy ending. My life is not a fairy tale. However, I may actually live happily ever after.

That is how I felt after my third year of doing the Arrowsmith program. I was having a lot easier time reading, retaining the information in my head, and analyzing the information. In fact, I became very good at analyzing things and understanding the main ideas and messages in books.

On the academic side of my homeschooling, I had an English teacher named Christy, who nurtured my love for reading. She said that I was like a brand new person. She was right.

I was able to keep math formulas in my head and I started to perform much better on math tests. I began to get A's in math, which was really weird for me because I never thought I could do that.

Things were very good at the beginning of my fourth year in the Arrowsmith program. And they got even better.

I continued with the various exercises such as phrases, clocks, tracing, and picture interpretation. Although my brain had improved significantly, it was not like the exercises were now totally easy.

Phrases, which required me to repeat back increasingly difficult and nonsensical phrases back to my teacher, was still quite tricky at the beginning of my fourth year. However, I had an incredible breakthrough moment late in that fourth year. I was at a very high difficulty level for the exercise, but I listened to this very hard phrase and I immediately got it. I was instantly able to repeat the phrase three times. For an hour, I kept doing these really hard phrases and instantly mastering them.

These phrases were so hard and difficult, but my brain was conquering them. At the end I started bawling because I was so happy. I had finally punched through this giant wall. It was like a blind person being able to see or a deaf person being able to hear. I had won.

I was doing really well on tracing, so the symbols I had to trace were becoming smaller and narrower. I eventually had to use a very tiny Japanese pencil to do the tracing. It was hard, but, of course, that also showed the great progress that I had made.

With clocks, I started the year reading clock faces with eight hands. By the end of my fourth year, I was reading 10-handed clocks. Further, I was reading these clocks very fast. I had to type almost instantly what each hand was telling me. And I did.

R-Think, the picture interpretation exercise, was no piece of cake for me. But, like in the other exercises, it got progressively easier for me as the fourth year rolled on.

The great progress I was making in the Arrowsmith exercises in my fourth year impacted my academics. I have already mentioned that I read 53 books during the summer between my third and fourth years in Arrowsmith. In my fourth year, I received a huge confidence booster.

I took a reading test that year when I was in the seventh grade. The results showed that I was reading at the 11th-grade level. I was so amazed and happy. I then started to read more difficult, challenging, high-school-level books.

In math, I was doing geometry. It was not my favorite or easiest subject, but not because my brain could not process things. Geometry was a challenge because it is simply a hard subject for the average seventh grader. It was not like there was a wall in my brain that prevented me from understanding the subject matter. So that by itself was a victory.

Overall, compared to how I entered the Arrowsmith program, I felt like going from being stuck in traffic in downtown San Francisco to driving in a Ferrari on an open freeway. Now everything seemed to be moving at lightning speed in my brain. Everything seemed to click. No more counting on fingers, no more forgetting instructions, no more offsetting strategies. It was great.

One of the other interesting transformations I experienced was that I felt calmer. Before, a lot of times I felt hyper, like I was bouncing off walls and had one too many espresso shots. Now, I was able to dial things down a notch, which was really nice.

Also, I did not feel sorry for myself. If I could not achieve something, I did not feel like I was going to be a failure the rest of my life. I had the confidence to know that if I made a mistake I would try again and get it right.

Whereas before I was able to train my brain my world seemed closed in, now the world seemed to open up for me.

My family was really proud of me. Not just for improving my brain, but for my persistence in sticking with the program and not giving up when things were tough and seeing results was difficult.

Perhaps the most rewarding thing that happened to me in my fourth year in the Arrowsmith program had nothing to do with my own individual progress. Rather, it had to do with giving to others.

Because I was able to conclude many of the exercises in my fourth year, reaching the highest difficulty levels, I was able to then help other students in our program. I could give them tips and strategies based on my own experience and on what I had learned.

The students I helped were not just kids. One of the students I was able to help was a young woman in her early twenties. She was from Ohio, and she and I were doing mostly the same exercises. At first, because I was 13 at the time, she thought I was just a young kid. But I was more advanced and farther along than she was, so I helped her with all the exercises.

For example, I would do phrases with her. I would say the phrase to her and she had to repeat the phrase back to me correctly three times. I would give her advice on how to remember the phrases. I was actually teaching her, and we started to build a relationship where I was more like a mentor for her even though she was significantly older than me. We would have meaningful conversations. She progressed really well. In the end, our age gap disappeared from our consciousness.

The older students said that I gave them hope because I was so young and because of how terrible things were for me when I first started the program. Adult students complimented me saying that the stories I told and the way I spoke made them forget that I was 13 years old. I was proof that for them that they could succeed, too.

That fourth year in Arrowsmith was the best conclusion I could ever have hoped for.

CHAPTER ELEVEN

The Medical School Director: Been There, Understand That
Lance Izumi

"I decided I wanted to be a massage therapist," said Dr. Anne Weisman, because "I knew what it was to suffer."

Indeed, she had suffered a lot. And through that suffering, she understands what Mia had to go through.

On the Fourth of July in 1999, Weisman nearly died in a horrendous car accident in the Lake Tahoe area.

All the injuries to her head resulted in severe traumatic brain injury.

Luckily, there was a woman two cars behind her who had just received her paramedic certification the day before, and upon seeing the accident pulled over to help.

And it was this woman, she says, "who called for the ambulance and the helicopter because she knew that I was dying."

On the helicopter, her heart had stopped, but the emergency crew was able to get it going again. After arriving in Reno, she was taken to a hospital intensive care unit and placed on life support.

"I was on life support for six days and in a coma," she recounted.

Not able to breathe on her own, she was intubated down her mouth and trachea with a flexible plastic tube to keep her alive and breathing.

"When I woke up from my coma six days later, I apparently, the story goes, pulled the intubation out of my body," she laughed, "and said a bad word."

She was able to breathe on her own again, but it would take much, much longer for her brain to heal.

Although she was conscious, she has only vague memories of what happened over the next several weeks, until "I remember waking up in my childhood bedroom and just like, you know, groggy, and looking around and thinking what am I doing here."

Indeed, she was faced with a very trying personal situation.

"So, I started and I had no short-term memory at that time," and because of her memory issues, "I became really fascinated with the human brain and I started to look up and read anything that I could get my hands on about severe traumatic brain injuries."

In fact, at the time, she really didn't know the true extent of her brain injury. Just a few years ago, she learned that part of her brain appeared to be missing based on scans done for her lower teeth.

Like Mia, Weisman's doctors were not optimistic about her future. Her doctors encouraged her to continue her education but believed that she was only going to be able to learn at a sixth-grade level.

To offset her short-term memory loss, she started keeping lists and calendars to give her points of reference when somebody asked her about her activities, and then she started taking classes.

Amazingly, she was eventually able to finish college and then initially pursue a career in public relations.

Yet, she felt, "I had this full recognition of just how badly my own body had been hurt, and I wanted to help people feel better."

She went on to win the Jefferson Award for Public Service in Las Vegas for her volunteer work with HIV and AIDS sufferers, and after talking with key people at the medical school at the University of Nevada at Las Vegas, she went on to do graduate work and eventually received her masters and Ph.D. in public health and social and behavioral health from UNLV.

With her academic credentials in hand, in 2015 Annie was appointed as director of wellness and integrative health at UNLV medical school. In that position, according to her university biography, she specializes in incorporating massage therapy and other integrative practices into the care and treatment of patients.

"I'm in charge of building wellness and integrative medicine curriculum throughout our medical students training," she says

She also exposes medical students to wellness and relaxation techniques so that they can take better care of themselves. Also, medical students are taught non-traditional techniques, such as the use of essential oils, hypnotherapy, massage therapy, and acupuncture, in order to better treat their future patients.

Given her own life's journey and her openness to non-traditional techniques, Weisman is perhaps uniquely positioned to appreciate what Mia went through and to give her personal and professional observations about Mia's journey.

Reacting to the Arrowsmith program that worked so well for Mia, Weisman said:

> I think it's great. I feel like we are alive at a time where people are really starting to look for alternatives. And even though our health-care system is embedded the way it is, our ed-

ucational system suffers similar struggles. I
think people are so hungry for a different way.
But I feel like the time is now.

Indeed, she feels, "we're just scratching the surface of our
potential in terms of what we're doing with our brains and our
brain health and our brain capacity."

Like Mia, Weisman says, "I remember feeling really deep
shame about my mental acuity and my mental state, so although my brain and mind were working, I felt really deficient
and embarrassed about that."

Mia telling her story, says Weisman, is important because
"I feel like all significant changes started with one person. The
more people learn about the Arrowsmith program and the
more people have hope again, they recognize that there are
things we can do individually and collectively to bring about
some healing."

"I feel like it will be a grassroots effort," she predicts, "it
will be something that people really help lead the change,
much like what we've seen in integrative medicine, where 20
years ago complementary and alternative medicine was really
pretty bastardized by [conventional] medicine."

"All human beings want to feel good and they want to be
understood," she points out, "and I think it's about educating
people that there are other ways; it's not black and white; and
there's no one path toward healing, but are many."

And if there is no one path necessarily in healing, there is
no one path in education as well.

Annie emphasizes the importance of equity. "I think
there's so much that goes into healing and us having the access
to these programs or parents that can homeschool us or send us
to different schools. I think that makes a difference."

Given Mia's bad experience at structured conventional
public and private schools, it is pertinent that Weisman, who
grew up as part of a large Irish Catholic family and attended
tradition-oriented parochial schools, observed: "For me, grow-

ing up in a traditional setting where everything was really laid out, there were uniforms, we were scheduled, and it was pretty black and white. I always had the rebel spirit within me and I also had the time and space to think there's got to be better ways."

For Mia, that better way was to be homeschooled and to access a non-traditional program like Arrowsmith that used a different paradigm than the conventional schools. Just as Dr. Anne Weisman overcame the effects of her brain injury through her own individual regimen, so Mia eventually overcame her brain and learning deficiencies through a regimen that addressed her individual situation. The ability to have choice cannot be understated.

One of the colleges Mia visited was Notre Dame University where Annie always wanted to attend. Weisman then says: "It makes me so happy to know parts of her journey and to know that she may end up where my heart was set on as a child and all the way through adolescence. I just think it's a really cool victory lap."

CHAPTER TWELVE
To Infinity and Beyond
Mia Giordano

After four years of the Arrowsmith program, I felt that my brain was like a big sponge that could soak up all this knowledge. Instead of being in a fog, where it seemed like information would just bounce off my brain, now I was full of questions because I knew that my brain could absorb the information needed to answer them.

I had reached a new phase in my life. Before, my brain and my future were clouded. Now everything seemed possible.

The big question was what kind of educational setting would best suit me for this new phase in my life? Should I continue the homeschooling that had worked so well for me from the fourth grade to the seventh grade? Or should I try something different?

One thing that I did miss while I was being homeschooled was going to school with my sister Cara. She and I have always been extremely close, not only in terms of age, less than two years, but as best friends. Going to school with her again would be wonderful.

Cara was going to a private school in the Bay Area called Synapse. My mom has always said that she believes that emotional quotient or EQ is more important than intelligence quotient or IQ. Synapse fit her belief.

Synapse was started in 2009 by two education innovators, Karen McCown and Anabel Jensen, who wanted to blend strong academics with social emotional development:

> They created a lab school that would showcase the impact of a program that fully integrates an emotional intelligence program and a robust constructivist curriculum. Karen and Anabel redefined education by combining the latest neuroscience research with social emotional learning and the practice of innovation.[58]

Given my background, it was, excuse the pun, a no-brainer for me to join Cara at Synapse. Going to school with Cara again was a wonderful bonus.

So, I started the eighth grade at Synapse. It turned out to be a great fit for me. I adjusted very quickly. After a week I was feeling very comfortable and dove right in.

The learning was done through working on projects. This more hands-on approach suited me better than just memorizing and repeating back information.

One of the really nice aspects of Synapse was something that they called advisories. The school would organize students into small groups and each group would have a teacher who would act as the group's advisor. The teacher would help students with anything from homework to advising them on projects. The advisories would meet at the beginning of the day and we would talk and discuss things for forty minutes. It was like a little family time before you started your day.

Of course, I took the usual academic classes: English, geometry, science, social studies and the like. It was really satisfying to be able to understand complex subject matter.

For example, I became really interested in Shakespeare. I picked up a copy of *Othello* and loved it. Then I read *Romeo and Juliet*.

Because of my newfound love of Shakespeare, my mom hired Mr. Ryan Dawson to tutor me in Shakespeare. Mr. Dawson had a great passion for the Bard and we read *Macbeth*, *Hamlet, Taming of the Shrew,* and *Cleopatra*.

He and I would read Shakespeare's plays together and then he would ask me questions to sharpen my analytical skills. We would often act out the plays as well. Even though the old-style language in the plays was a challenge, it did not prevent me from reading the plays, understanding them, and analyzing them. It felt awesome.

Mr. Dawson said that he was really impressed by my abilities. Because I did not get hung up on the hard vocabulary in the plays, he said that I was able to see the bigger picture and meaning that Shakespeare was trying to get across.

One of my breakthrough moments came when Mr. Dawson and I were reading *Macbeth* together. An important theme in *Macbeth* involves temptation. Macbeth is constantly being tempted by power and ends up committing many terrible acts because he gives in to temptation.

Since I am Catholic, I could see the similarity and differences between the temptation of Macbeth and the temptation of Jesus. Macbeth was tempted by the witches with power, just like Jesus was tempted by Satan with power during Jesus' forty days in the desert. But unlike Macbeth, Jesus refused the temptations of Satan.

While people say that money is the root of all evil, Catholics believe that temptation is the root of all evil because all the deadly sins flow from temptation.

Catholics also believe that people have the free will to give in to temptation or to refuse temptation. Even though the witches tell Macbeth about things that may happen in the future, Macbeth still had the free will to decide against temptation, but instead he used his free will to give in to temptation.

Mr. Dawson said that he understood that *Macbeth* had certain Catholic overtones, but he was really impressed by my analysis of *Macbeth* using the Catholic view of temptation. He said that although he was supposed to be the expert on Shakespeare, I actually showed him a new way of reading *Macbeth*. He could now see that *Macbeth* could be a Catholic morality play in disguise. It was a moment, he said, when the student became the master. For me, it was a triumph being able to convey my thoughts so well that I was able to influence someone whom I greatly respected.

Another area of clarity came in the field of politics and complex political issues. I remember creating a presentation on the 2016 election, which went against the thoughts of many of my classmates. I was confident in my arguments and in the end, events showed that I was right. This episode boosted my confidence a lot and I really felt that I could take on the world after that. It was like giving sight to a blind person, who could now see all the colors of the earth.

Because of my new confidence, I was able to participate in healthy debates with others. I once had a debate with one of my teachers who said that America's founding fathers wanted a two-party system of government. I countered by pointing out that the founders actually did not want a two-party system. He said that I was wrong, but confidently I held my ground and presented evidence supporting my position, such as John Adams saying, "There is nothing which I dread so much as a division of the republic into two great parties."[59] When he saw my evidence, my teacher said, "Well, I didn't know that." I was proud of myself for being confident enough to stick to my guns and debate my teacher when most students would have backed down.

In fact, because I was homeschooled, it turned out that I was more knowledgeable about subjects like history than my fellow students. Therefore I was able to have more in-depth discussions, which helped me and others learn as well. Also, when I was homeschooled my mom used the Socratic method to teach me. The Socratic method draws the argument out of you and makes you justify your statements with evidence and facts.

Since Synapse had a freer learning environment, I was able to use the skills that I had honed to participate in deeper discussions. When I thought about how I was before my brain re-training, I was amazed at how my life had changed. Before, I would not be able to touch really hard subjects and issues, not because they were too complex or difficult, but because I simply would not be able to hear and process the information in my brain. In contrast, now I was beating my teachers in debates. What a change.

My brain was processing a wealth of information outside of school, too. I was listening and watching radio and television shows on current events and was able to process the information and arguments that I heard. My mind opened up and I was able to grow as a person and develop my beliefs.

My changed brain also reduced my anxiety when faced with hard subjects.

Like many other students, I hated geometry. In the past, when faced with a difficult subject I would develop anxiety about not being able to get the right answer. I would get paralyzed. Now, even with a subject I hated, I could work through the problems, achieve success, build greater confidence, and remove the anxiety. That emotional reaction to difficult material disappeared. However, even a changed brain couldn't make me love geometry.

My Arrowsmith exercises ended up helping me in my art class. Prior to Arrowsmith, I could not draw well at all. To get an image onto paper was very hard for me. There was a disconnect between my head and my hand. The tracing exercise helped re-connect my head to my hand, as did the clock exercises. I always liked art, but now I could do art.

On the social side, Synapse was a great place for me. Not only did I have my sister there, but I was able to make lots of friends. The school encouraged family involvement, so there were lots of family days that brought the school community together.

So, I did really well in my eighth-grade year at Synapse, both academically and socially.

Because Synapse was a K-8 school, it served as a perfect stepping stone for me to then go on to high school in the ninth grade. And I was ready and excited for high school.

Unlike the choice of Synapse for my eighth grade, however, choosing a high school was not so clear. Various factors would have to be considered.

My mom wanted an education option that emphasized self-directed learning, where I could dive deep into subjects. Homeschooling fit that bill and we almost went that route. Then we discovered Design Tech charter high school.

Design Tech is a unique school that brings together the philosophy of design thinking and combines it with the tools of technology. According to the school:

> 'DESIGN' - refers to d.tech's design thinking program. It offers applied practice in a problem-solving method developed at the Stanford Design School and shared through their K-12 Lab program. When applied to real-world challenges, this develops self-efficacy, collaborative confidence and emotional intelligence. Students learn to adopt feedback as useful and actionable information, and embrace the idea that effort is needed to push through anticipated set-backs.

> 'TECH' - refers to students learning to handle new technology comfortably. It's common for entering high schoolers to know either very little, or a lot about technology. Students become accustomed to 3-D printers, laser cutters and design software as potential tools to express and realize their ideas. Over time, they gain confidence in applying whatever tools are needed to accomplish their academic and de-

sign goals. This confidence and open-mind-edness remains with them even as the resources around them evolve.[60]

The school literally started in a garage but is now located on the business campus of the Oracle corporation in the Bay Area. When I visited the school, I immediately knew that this was where I wanted to go.

The students, who were from incredibly diverse backgrounds, were my type of people. The teachers, who mentored students through daily advisories (like at Synapse) and offered personalized instruction, were my kind of educators. The school culture was so freeing, with students wanting to learn, discover, and find solutions.

One of the key principles of design thinking is empathy. In a project in which you are trying to find a solution to a problem, you have to understand the needs of the user of your solution. You need to empathize with them.

For example, when I was working on a project to make lunchtime better for students at the school, we interviewed students to understand their viewpoints and their needs. Based on these interviews, we were able to design better benches for the students that were cheap and comfortable. Since we had the facilities and tools to produce the benches, we could put them around the school.

This quality of empathy was natural to me. I had empathized with the kids starting off in the Arrowsmith program who felt like they had no hope. I knew exactly what they were going through. I knew what they were feeling. I knew it was a struggle. Since I felt like I was their beacon of hope because I had been in their shoes, but now look how I turned out.

Design Tech pushes students to take risks. When you take risks, sometimes you fail. But unlike before when I was paralyzed with the fear of failure, now I recognize that mistakes are part of learning and I am able to look at those mistakes and figure out how to correct them. So, failure is really an opportunity to make things better.

As I write these chapters reflecting on my life, I am still at Design Tech. I am having an amazing time at this amazing school. And perhaps the most amazing thing to realize is how my life is so changed over what it had been before.

Without the brain training I received through the Arrowsmith program, I would not be the person I am today. I would not be able to write and communicate with those of you who are reading this book. In fact, because of the combination of low self-esteem and physical inabilities, I would probably only be able to communicate with a small circle of people. I would not be the extroverted and outgoing person I am today. Life would have been hard all the time--a constant struggle. And that struggle would have left me constantly exhausted because that effort drains you of all your energy.

Looking back on my journey, I have to ask why anyone would want to live his or her life with a learning disability struggling day after day coping with the most basic parts of existence.

Yet, the answer to that question involves not just a person's determination, it also involves the choices that people can make for themselves.

If my family did not have the ability to make choices in my education that would meet my specific needs, right now I would be just an older version of third-grade Mia—stuck in time and definitely depressed.

Without trying these different avenues of learning, I would not have found out what really worked for me. In fact, the most valuable thing that I can take away from my life so far is that I learned exactly what I need to do to learn my best. But in order for me to find that out, I needed to be able to choose the education that best helped me.

If my mom just put me in a regular public school and said, "You're on your own," I would never have thrived as a person. In fact, I most likely would have failed. I would never have known what was my best learning style and what environment I needed to learn the best.

For me, it was not a regular public school or even a really good private school. A mixture of homeschooling and an innovative charter school was what worked best for me. But to discover that golden mixture required that my family have the ability to choose among different education options and not be stuck with a single, one-size-fits-all alternative.

My mom says that she wants parents of children with learning disabilities to not settle for being the hamster on the wheel of the conventional education system. She tells the story of being at a fundraising dinner and hearing a teacher who had lived her life with a learning disability.

This teacher said that she accepted her learning disability. It took her three years to finally pass the math class she needed to get her teaching credential. When she said that, people started clapping and weeping with tears of joy for her. My mom, however, was crying with tears of sadness.

This teacher had wasted three years of her life. As Barbara Arrowsmith-Young says, just because you have a learning disability does not mean you have to live with it. Children, especially, should not have to waste years of their life trying to achieve something that they could achieve much quicker if they had the opportunity to choose a better way to learn.

Good science and better ways to learn do not mean anything if you cannot choose them. The Arrowsmith program works, but if my family could not choose it, then it might as well have never existed.

My journey, therefore, is not only about my personal struggles and ultimate triumph, but it is also about the much bigger issue of giving all children the same choices that I had. I was able to succeed because my family had choices in education. Only when all families have the same ability to make choices will all children have the chance to succeed that I had.

I am so thankful for everything that has happened to me because it has made me the person I am today.

When I look at the years ahead, I see limitless possibilities, whereas my life before was defined by seemingly endless limitations.

In the Disney "Toy Story" movies, the wonderful character Buzz Lightyear's trademark line is, "To infinity and beyond!" That is how I see my future and it is a great feeling.

CHAPTER THIRTEEN
Why We Need Choice in Education
Lance Izumi

I n America's shifting educational landscape, says author and homeschooling expert Kerry McDonald, "the students and parents are the ones who are really helpless to guide the process of education," with the result that schools "are unable to be more tailored to individual students."

In her 2019 book *Unschooled: Raising Curious, Well-Educated Children Outside the Conventional Classroom,* McDonald notes how her own four children are very different from each other, with significant developmental differences, such as talking, walking and reading at different ages.

"How could an age-segregated, one-size-fits-all system of mass schooling," wondered McDonald, "possibly appreciate and accommodate the vast diversity of the human experience?"[61]

In an interview for this book, McDonald said that her first experience with homeschooling came in her senior year in college when she did a research project on a homeschooling family that she shadowed.

"This was the late 1990s," she recalled, and "homeschooling had just become legally recognized in all 50 states just a few years prior in 1993, so it was still relatively new, and I remember just being completely enchanted by seeing the way this child was learning and seeing how curious and confident and articulate she was."

In contrast, that same semester, she was doing student teaching in a local public elementary school, "which was really much more focused around this kind of conventional command and control approach to education, and so it really wasn't until that moment that I saw this difference between a different way of learning and the conventional way of learning that I had grown up with having attended K-12 public schools."

It was a defining and life-changing time for McDonald, which "ultimately led me to graduate school and education policy at Harvard and becoming more and more interested in education choice, parental choice, and innovative education models."

In her book, McDonald says, "As Americans, we seem genuinely willing to embrace—even fight for—freedom for most people on our planet." Yet, "we place children in increasingly restrictive learning environments, at ever-earlier ages and for much longer portions of their day and year than at any other time in our history." Further:

> We place the vast majority of children in schooling environments that are much more controlling and unpleasant and unhealthy than we grown-ups would accept in our own lives and workplaces. We allow children's bodies and thoughts to be managed by others, and we dismiss institutional side effects, like bullying, obesity, anxiety, and depression, a decline in

gross motor skills, and a rise in ADHD and other health disorders. Actions that would be criminal in our adult workplace are tolerated and expected in our children's schooling.[62]

"It is no wonder," she observes, "that under these oppressive institutional conditions—characteristic of the rise of the Industrial Age—most children have the life force drained out of them."[63]

Since McDonald first became interested in homeschooling, the number of homeschooled American children has skyrocketed.

According to federal statistics, in 1999, there were 850,000 children who were being homeschooled. By 2016, that number had doubled to 1.7 million.

Today, McDonald says, "homeschooling now has about 2 million young people in the K-to-12 age range in the United States."

Many people associate homeschooling with parents who want to give their children religious instruction, but federal data shows that larger percentages of homeschool parents cite poor school environment and dissatisfaction with instruction rather than religious issues as top reasons why they decided to homeschool their children.

Indeed, the rise in homeschooling is occurring as more and more parents are questioning the cookie-cutter conventional schools.

"I think what we're seeing even more so in the past couple of decades," McDonald explains, "is the increasing standardization of schooling, with young people now spending increasingly more time in these standardized learning environments" and "being tested on a very rigid curriculum." In the process, she says, many children are being harmed.

In response to this one-size-fits-all conventional schooling, "parents are looking for choices" because "we live in this moment of incredible variety and choice and freedom in so many areas of our life, and yet when you look at education, and particularly the default education, where most kids attend an assigned district school tied to a zip code, there's very limited choice for so many families."

Parents are starting to wise up, however, as they notice that they have lots of options in almost every area of life, and yet have so few options in their children's education.

McDonald believes parents "are looking for much more tailored, personalized approaches," similar to personalization in medicine and nutrition.

Yet much of the conventional school systems are geared to schooling versus education. McDonald defines the difference between the two concepts saying, "the key difference between school and education is that schooling is training people to do certain things in certain ways at certain times, and education is the product of a beautiful broad process of learning the skills, customs and tools of your culture, so that you're able to live a fulfilling meaningful life that contributes to society and then enables you to reach your full potential."

"Education," therefore, "is much more focused on individual active human flourishing."

When the public common schools were established in the 19th century, they were "very much focused on shaping young people to a common pattern," since it was based on a Prussian model "that really valued conformity, obedience, regimentation, and the process of moving from one grade to the next." But our world today, McDonald emphasizes, is not the world of the 19th Century:

> Parents are saying, well, that might have been okay for the rise of the Industrial Revolution, but we're in a moment where we are well into the innovation era, where skills and jobs are changing so quickly, that we can't rely on this archaic system of one-size-fits-all schooling. We have to be more agile. We have to have many different options and lots of experimentation in education that conventional schooling can't possibly provide.

That is why, McDonald says, "Mia's example is so important, because it shows that when parents are able to take control, whether through homeschooling, private schools or even public charter schools, there is that opportunity for customization for parental control and for innovation that is really difficult to implement in a conventional mass schooling system."

McDonald's observation has proven true in innumerable instances across the country.

For example, when two parents of autistic children found that the regular New York City public schools did not offer the innovative and effective instruction and education services they believed that their children needed, they used New York's state charter-school law to create New York City Autism Charter School.

Julie Fisher, the executive director of NYC Autism Charter School, mirrors McDonald's thinking when she pointed out:

> I think the charter-school movement has pushed the envelope in terms of thinking outside of the box. What you see when you look at autism education is the need for looking at the individual. Tailoring things in a way that . . . a general curriculum—a cookie-cutter approach—wouldn't allow for.[64]

Politico writer Eliza Shapiro observed that NYC Autism "could only exist as a charter, outside of the bureaucratic strictures of traditional public schools where teachers are free to adapt to a child's specific needs in real time."[65]

And just as NYC Autism punctures the argument that charter schools do not address the issue of special-needs children, so McDonald points out that homeschooling can often better address the issues of children with diagnosed special needs.

In fact, she says, "there's a lot of young people on the autism spectrum whose parents often remove them from school or choose not to send them to begin with, because these kids have brilliant minds and different ways of learning and so it should be supported and facilitated in ways that they don't believe the conventional school system can."

In her book, she says that conventional schools not only emphasize control, order, and conformity, but "the increasing time and intensity of schoolstuffs at earlier ages pushes them to the very limits of their adaptability."[66]

Thus, "More young children are exhibiting school-related behavioral and attention disorders now than ever before, and they are more likely to be treated with potent psychotropic medications for what are often normal childhood actions that can become pathologized within an early forced schooling context."[67] Yet, these increasing diagnoses and treatments may be due to the impact of conventional schooling on children rather than on something inherently wrong with these children:

> Curious about mounting data showing possible correlations between school attendance and ADHD diagnoses, psychologist Dr. Peter Grey conducted his own informal, online survey of children who left conventional schooling for homeschooling or other forms of alternative education. He found that for children previously labeled ADHD, often with related anxiety issues, children's behavioral and emotional problems were dramatically reduced, or disappeared altogether, and their overall learning improved when they left conventional schooling. Results were particularly positive when children engaged self-directed education, or unschooling, where they had more freedom and control over their own learning. Dr. Grey concludes that ADHD is essentially a "failure to adapt to the conditions of standard schooling."[68]

Remember that Mia's conventional school had insinuated that she had an attention disorder, which she did not have.

McDonald recounts the story of Tracy Ventola, an elementary school teacher, whose mother was a teacher and whose father was a public-school special-education teacher for 30 years. Yet, the inability of the conventional schools to meet the needs of her daughter caused Tracy to re-think her ideas about education:

> Like so many parents who make the leap from schooling to unschooling, Tracy gradually realized that the problems her older daughter was experiencing in school (first in a traditional preschool and then in a more progressive private school) were a result of schooling and not of her daughter. "When she started preschool, my already shy girl got even quieter," says Tracy. "She pulled further into herself, to the point that she stopped talking. Her reaction to school earned her a diagnosis of selective mutism. School had the opposite effect on my friend's son. Her incredibly bright, super-verbal, high-energy kid got louder; he went further outside himself and therefore has been diagnosed with ADHD. There is nothing wrong with either of these children. They are simply coping differently with the stress of school."[69]

McDonald reported that when Tracy and her husband pulled their daughter out of conventional school and started to homeschool her, they said that the results were astonishing. Their daughter became happy, talkative, and engaged. Rather than the stressful environment of the conventional school classroom, the parents created a slow peaceful rhythm, which resulted in their daughter growing more confident and extroverted.[70]

Tracy's daughter became interested in drawing, making art, and became a voracious reader. And the girl once diagnosed with selective mutism now has a growing passion for theatre and regularly performs live in front of large public audiences.

"For Tracy," says McDonald, "trusting her parenting instincts enabled her to question the prevailing trend of labeling children for alleged disorders that are often just extreme adaptive responses to the artificiality of school."[71]

In her interview for this book, McDonald observed, "many parents with children who have special needs are the ones who are opting out of the conventional classrooms for homeschooling and other alternatives to school because they see the opportunity to customize an education and to tailor learning to that individual child's unique interest, gifts, skills, and talents."

The result is a "critical mass of today's homeschooling families that are homeschooling young people with special needs."

She notes the interesting case of Florida, "which is seeing a large increase in the homeschooling population and is also a leader in school-choice mechanisms, like education savings accounts." She points specifically to Florida's Gardiner Scholarship Program that gives special-needs children the opportunity to receive an education savings account funded by the state and administered by an approved scholarship funding organization.

Under the Gardiner program, parents can use these funds to pay for a variety of educational services, including private school tuition, tutoring, online education, home education, curriculum, therapy, postsecondary educational institutions in Florida and other defined services.[72]

The Gardiner Scholarship Program is contained in sections 393.063 and 1002.385 of Florida Statutes. Pertinent rules for the program include no income limit, no enrollment cap, state and national testing of the child if appropriate, and various specified diagnosed special needs. [73]

The estimated average amount in the Gardiner savings accounts for 2018-19 is around $10,400. Eleven percent of Florida students are eligible for the program and more than 11,900 students participated in the program as of Fall 2018.[74]

The school-choice organization EdChoice points out that while Florida's McKay scholarship is the nation's largest voucher program for students with special needs, the Gardiner education savings accounts "give parents access to educational therapy, tutoring and online learning programs, which are inaccessible through a traditional voucher program."[75]

Dr. Anne Weisman points out that when it comes to aspects of homeschooling there is "a huge issue with equity."

"I think we face a ton of barriers in terms of equity," she observed. For instance, "Mia and myself are in positions to have families that could help us."

"I don't think it can be understated," she emphasized, "there's so much that goes into healing and us having the access to these programs or parents that can homeschool us or send us to different schools which makes a difference."

She is right, which is why the Gardiner program is so important. It delivers the equity that is necessary to ensure fair opportunities for all special-needs children by giving less affluent parents the ability to access programs such as the one that helped Mia and others that are helping many other children.

For example, Arely Burgos and her husband left Puerto Rico with their young son Omar, who has autism. The family located to Florida and used the state's Gardiner Scholarship to send Omar to a Montessori school, where he sees therapists twice a week. Arely says:

> The Gardiner Scholarship is the best thing to happen to [Omar]. We have seen tremendous progress in Omar the last two years. The school is fantastic and the therapists are fabulous. We sure make a great team! There is nothing in Puerto Rico that would make me go back again.

It breaks my heart to know there are families out there who are unable to enjoy the same benefits from Gardiner.

As a parent of a special-needs child, I know what they are going through — the stress and the uncertainly. You worry about your child's future if they can't live by themselves. What happens to them if you die? What if you don't have enough money to help them? I'm moved to tears thinking of the services they need but cannot afford.

Gardiner not only helps provide these students with the tools to succeed — it gives their families peace of mind that they will not be left behind.[76]

A program like the Gardiner Scholarship, therefore, balances the equity playing field for all families.

Florida Governor Ron DeSantis has called the Gardiner program "a proven success." The Florida legislature has increased funding for the Gardiner savings accounts, thus "providing even more students with special needs access to the educational services they need," and Florida lawmakers "also expanded the program to include additional disabilities, as well as 4- and 5-year-old students deemed at risk for developmental delays."[77]

The added funding, which raises total Gardiner funding to $148 million, should increase the number of Gardiner scholarship recipients in 2020 to more than 14,000.

Patrick Gibbons, research fellow at EdChoice, has noted: "The Gardiner program serves students with specific special needs including autism, Down Syndrome and spina bifida. Students on the autism spectrum make up about 63 percent of the Gardiner student population."[78]

In its evaluation of the Gardiner Scholarship Program, EdChoice observes:

Notably, Florida's [Gardiner education savings account] program is administered by approved nonprofit organizations that reimburse parents for approved expenses. One nonprofit has developed a payment process for parents who cannot make purchases out of pocket. It is encouraging to see Florida take an innovative approach to delivering services and educational choice programs to more families. Florida's nonprofit approach to ESA administration provides a good policy example to states considering ESA programs because such organizations have greater autonomy and flexibility than state bureaucracies and are primarily dedicated to ensuring that children have access to the educational options they need.[79]

McDonald says that many parents are using the Gardiner education savings accounts to "homeschool their child, often in conjunction with tutoring and other programs and activities that can help their particular child."

"So, I think there's a lot of synergy between educational choice and homeschooling, particularly as it relates to special needs children," she notes with approval, "which I think will just give parents so many more options going forward."

Stacey, a mother whose special-needs son Liam is the recipient of a Gardiner savings-account scholarship, says:

The fact that the scholarship is personalized to each child is amazing because as a parent with a child with special needs there are so many therapies and educational needs for the child that become very expensive. I like that we can choose where we want to use that money to help better our children. So, when I found out about this scholarship program, I was over-the-moon excited.[80]

She says that Liam is now reading at grade level, which is helping his speech, the length of the sentences he is able to say, and the overall level of his communication.

"This is such a game-changer for parents of children with special needs," she says.[81]

It should be noted that Florida is one of the states where the Arrowsmith Program is available at a number of private schools in Miami, Jacksonville, Ocala, Davie, and Winter Park.

For example, the Access School in Davie says that it is the "only cognitive school in Florida," with the motto: "Building the brain to give your child the advantage."

The Access School offers the Arrowsmith Program in grades 1-6 in order to address students with dyslexia, dysgraphia, dyscalculia, and problems in reading, comprehension, writing, math, working and visual memory, attention, auditory processing, auditory memory, logical reasoning, and nonverbal learning. After an initial assessment to identify a student's strengths and weaknesses, the school develops a personalized program for the student and implements it after it is reviewed by the student's parents or guardians.[82]

"Upon completing two to three years of programming," says the Access School, "a student can capitalize on their increased learning capacities without compensating." Further, "Weak cognitive areas will become strong and strong cognitive areas will become stronger."[83]

Zack was a student at the Access School who entered the school with a myriad of cognitive weaknesses including motor symbol sequencing such miscopying and misreading, symbol relations such as difficulty reading an analog clock and reversing letters, and object recognition such as remembering faces and recalling the visual details of pictures. Because of his cognitive weaknesses and his associated learning dysfunctions, he hated school. [84]

According to his parents, "Difficulties in school transcended into poor behavior and frustration at home," but, "After having the public school system fail us, we were introduced to the Access School."[85]

The Arrowsmith Program was definitely a draw for his parents: "The programming and approach are completely different, certainly not conventional, but there was a definite logic to make us investigate this program further."[86]

After going through the Arrowsmith Program, his parents were overjoyed with the results for their son. "We see the total difference," they said. He "is now more mature, he does not come home frustrated and his behavior has improved." [87]

His areas of cognitive weakness were strengthened and his learning abilities improved. In the view of his parents, "The small class environment and the neuroplastic programming at Access has been crucial."[88]

What is important to point out, in terms of McDonald's recommendations, is that the Access School is an approved institution for Gardiner and McKay Scholarship recipients.

Again, Florida's scholarship programs guarantee the type of equity and access that concerned Weisman.

Speaking specifically to Mia's case and her experience in conventional schools, McDonald says:

> My first reaction is anger. And I feel bad for the child and the parents who are told this information from experts and educators. I think, again, that's where these sorts of education choice mechanisms can be particularly beneficial to children with special needs, because they can provide access to these kinds of programs like Arrowsmith for children like Mia outside the conventional school.

Addressing the fact that Mia was the victim of bullying at school because of her special needs, McDonald observes:

There's definitely an increase in interest in homeschooling and other kinds of alternatives to school and education choice more broadly related to bullying and safety concern in conventional schools. Bullying is really tragic, because if you look at where bullying typically occurs, it's in places where people can't speak. So, it's rampant, for example, in prisons and in schools because you have to be there under legal threat of force. And so, I think the key is to give people, young people included, more opportunities to engage in those situations. If you think about it as adults, we would never tolerate that kind of bullying in our workplace. We would work towards trying to alleviate the situation and if we couldn't, we would quit. For some reason, we expect young people to tolerate bullying in a way that we would never tolerate in our own adult lives. And really, the only solution is to provide more opportunities to exit these kinds of oppressive environments.

Looking towards the future, McDonald says, "I'm really optimistic about the future of homeschooling, unschooling in particular, and educational freedom more broadly," especially given "that technology is driving much of this change and it will continue to lead in change in education and certainly in homeschooling and unschooling."

Homeschooling will be "a platform for education innovation, as it encourages more parents and entrepreneurial educators to create new learning centers or new types of schools and new software programs, all of which will really challenge this dominant type of conventional schooling."

Further, "homeschooling, because of its freedom and flexibility, and because it legally puts parents back in charge of a child's education, is well positioned to be the launch pad for many of these innovations in education."

The world is changing quickly, she says, "often because of technological advancement, that we really have to be looking beyond a conventional classroom to meet the realities of the 21st century." Parents and visionary educators know this, "and I think education will change because of that."

A Florida parent sums it all up: "The school-choice issue is not about public versus private; it's about choice. It's about knowing what works well for my family and being able to make that choice for them."[89]

EPILOGUE

Lance Izumi

This book started off with a prologue from Mia about the world before her. We now end with some thoughts about the world in light of her story.

In the few years of her life, Mia Giordano has lived through an incredible rollercoaster of emotions from sadness and joy, failure and achievement, and hopelessness and optimism. She has gone from being trapped in a cocoon of limitations to being poised for greatness. She is truly an inspiration.

Barbara Arrowsmith-Young knows Mia and says: "Mia really deeply touched my heart because the struggles she described were exactly the struggles I had. When I meet somebody like Mia it's like they are in my soul. It deeply, deeply, deeply touches my heart because I lived that journey and I know the pain and the suffering."

She says that it takes incredible courage to do what Mia did:

> I think fundamentally this work alleviates human suffering. I am so profoundly moved when I meet someone like Mia who has the

courage to step into this work because even though we can say that it's going to work, does she know that? She's probably tried other things that maybe haven't worked for her, so I am moved by her courage to go into this unknown territory.

I provided that program, but Mia is the one that stepped into that and did the hard work. Here she is at the other end of that, this beautiful human being who is engaged in the world. And I just think, "Wow." This is why I get up every morning and sometimes face these incredible challenges, like some of these educators who say you're crazy and you can't do this. That is why we do what we do. It is for the possibility of different futures [for people like Mia], which she has. And she was the engineer in her life that caused these changes.

"I am just humbled," Barbara says with emotion, "when I see what a remarkable human being she is."

Mia's journey, however, is not just the story of the personal triumph of one remarkable young woman. Rather, her story should serve as a call to action. Every child in America should have the same opportunity to succeed, which means that all parents should have the ability to choose the best education option for their children.

Arrowsmith-Young recognizes the importance of the broader need saying that she is in this fight "for all the Mias in the world who can be transformed in the way Mia was transformed."

Dr. Greg Rose says that even though he is a supporter of public schools, "one size does not fit all."

Mia's mother, Christine, says it is wrong "to say that you have to go to a one-size-fits-all school, and this is the card you have been dealt, and you have to learn to live with it."

On the contrary, she says, "It's important for parents to feel that they are in control of their children's learning, and as parents we should be allowed to look at the menu and choose."

Education is like a highway, says Christine, and parents and their children "want to try this road or that road." But the important point is that they should have the power to get off a bad road and turn onto a better one.

"It's very sad when I hear parents who don't know what's available to them," laments Christine. "We have an opportunity here in the United States to access other options."

Arrowsmith-Young says that giving parents and their children real education choices is "essential and critical."

"Parents," she says, "should have the option or the right to say this is the program that's going to benefit my child and the current education system is just not capable."

Speaking to equity, she emphasizes that no child should be denied access to programs of their choice that work for them because of finances.[90]

However, as Kerry McDonald points out, accessing those options will be realistic for many parents only if good public policy promoting educational choice is enacted, as has occurred in Florida, Arizona, and a few other states.

Sadly, there are millions of children in America who are being left behind because their parents do not have the ability to access the educational options that would work best for them. These parents may not have the financial means to choose alternative educational options, or they may live in states where educational choice tools are inadequate or non-existent. Their inability to choose then results in those supplying the educational choices, such as Arrowsmith, to decide against entering the education marketplace.

There is a reason why the Arrowsmith program is offered at schools in Florida, where the state's Gardiner and McKay scholarships make the program affordable for parents, and not in states that do not have similar educational choice tools.

As usual, Mia says it best:

> My journey, therefore, is not only about my personal struggles and ultimate triumph, but it is also about the much bigger issue of giving all children the same choices that I had. I was able to succeed because my family had choices in education. Only when all families have the same ability to make choices will all children have the chance to succeed that I had.

Mia's journey of change, success, and happiness should not be the story of just one young woman, but the story of millions of children. Only through enlightened public policy will that journey for America's children become a reality.

ENDNOTES

1   Barbara Arrowsmith-Young, *The Woman Who Changed Her Brain* (New York, NY: Free Press, 2012), p. 4.
2   Ibid.
3   See https://radiopaedia.org/articles/brodmann-areas?lang=us
4   Barbara Arrowsmith-Young, "Definition of a Learning Dysfunction," January 1996, available at https://arrowsmithschool.org/definition-of-a-learning-dysfunction/
5   Ibid.
6   Ibid.
7   Ibid.
8   In addition, "for math learning, the left superior longitudinal fasciculus (SLF) and its connections with frontal cortex and both parental and temporal cortex are of great importance." Rachel C. Weber, et al, "Interpreting the preliminary outcomes of the Arrowsmith Programme: a neuroimaging and behavioural study," *Learning: Research and Practice*, pp. 2-3, available at https://arrowsmithschool.org/wp-content/uploads/2019/10/Interpreting-the-preliminary-outcomes-of-the-arrowsmith-Programme-a-neuroimaging-and-behavioural-study.pdf
9   Barbara Arrowsmith-Young, "Definition of a Learning Dysfunction," January 1996, available at https://arrowsmithschool.org/definition-of-a-learning-dysfunction/
10 Ibid.
11 Ibid.
12 Rachel C. Weber, et al, "Interpreting the preliminary outcomes of the Arrowsmith Programme: a neuroimaging and behavioural study," *Learning: Research and Practice*, p. 3, available at https://arrowsmithschool.org/wp-content/uploads/2019/10/Interpreting-the-preliminary-outcomes-of-the-arrowsmith-Programme-a-neuroimaging-and-behavioural-study.pdf
13 Ibid.
14 Ibid.
15 See https://www.readingrockets.org/helping/target/phonologicalphonemic
16 "How Does Sleep Apnea Impact the Brain," Advanced Sleep Medicine, Inc., available at https://www.sleepdr.com/the-sleep-blog/how-does-sleep-apnea-impact-the-brain/
17 See https://slingerland.org/Approach
18 Barbara Arrowsmith-Young, *The Woman Who Changed Her Brain* (New York, NY: Free Press, 2012), p. 5.
19 Barbara Arrowsmith-Young, *The Woman Who Changed Her Brain* (New York, NY: Free Press, 2012), p. 203.
20 Ibid, p. 9.

21   Duncan Banks, "What is brain plasticity and why is it so important," *The Conversation,* April 4, 2016, available at https://theconversation. com/what-is-brain-plasticity-and-why-is-it-so-important-55967

22   Ibid.

23   Barbara Arrowsmith-Young, *The Woman Who Changed Her Brain* (New York, NY: Free Press, 2012), p. 33,

24   Ibid.

25   Ibid, p. 35.

26   Ibid.

27   Rachel C. Weber, et al, "Interpreting the preliminary outcomes of the Arrowsmith Programme: a neuroimaging and behavioural study," *Learning: Research and Practice,* p. 4-5, available at https://arrowsmith-school.org/wp-content/uploads/2019/10/Interpreting-the-prelim-inary-outcomes-of-the-arrowsmith-Programme-a-neuroimag-ing-and-behavioural-study.pdf

28   Ibid, p. 5. For a good explanation of the Arrowsmith Program's 19 different learning dysfunctions, see "The 19 Learning Dysfunctions," The Access School, available at http://www.accessschool.net/DOC percent2019 percent20LDs percent20PDF.pdf and Barbara Arrowsmith-Young, *The Woman Who Changed Her Brain* (New York, NY: Free Press, 2012), pp. 217-223.

29   See https://arrowsmithschool.org/background/

30   See https://arrowsmithschool.org/participating-sites/

31   Ibid.

32   Barbara Arrowsmith-Young, *The Woman Who Changed Her Brain* (New York, NY: Free Press, 2012), p. 34.

33   Rachel C. Weber, et al, "Interpreting the preliminary outcomes of the Arrowsmith Programme: a neuroimaging and behavioural study," *Learning: Research and Practice,* p. 15 and p. 19, available at https:// arrowsmithschool.org/wp-content/uploads/2019/10/Interpret-ing-the-preliminary-outcomes-of-the-arrowsmith-Programme-a-neu-roimaging-and-behavioural-study.pdf

34   Hanna Kubas, Jessica Carmichael, Kim Fitzer, and James Hale, "Effects of the Arrowsmith Program on Academic Performance: A Pilot Study," University of Calgary, 2014, available at http://www. arrowsmithschool.org/wp-content/uploads/2017/03/Kubas-CPA-2014-Final-June3.pdf

35   Ibid.

36   Kim Fitzer, Hanna Kubas, Jessica Carmichael, Howard Eaton, and James Hale, "A Brain-Based Intervention Program That Changes Cognition: Implications for Academic Achievement," University of Calgary, 2014, available at https://arrowsmithschool.org/wp-content/ uploads/2016/12/brainbased-intervention.pdf

37   See "Arrowsmith Program Research Summary 2019," Arrowsmith Program, 2019, available at https://arrowsmithschool.org/wp-con-tent/uploads/2019/10/Arrowsmith-Program-Research-Summa-ry-2019-Web-2.pdf

38 See https://www.sciencedirect.com/topics/psychology/cognitive-functioning

39 See https://arrowsmithschool.org/descriptions-of-learning-dysfunctions-addressed/

40 Ibid.

41 Ibid.

42 Ibid.

43 Ibid.

44 Howard Eaton, "Learning to Read a Clock Face," May 2018, available at http://howardeaton.com/2018/05/learning-how-to-read-a-clock-face/

45 See https://www.mayoclinic.org/diseases-conditions/dyslexia/symptoms-causes/syc-20353552

46 Mark Milke, "School Choice in Canada: Lessons for America," Heritage Foundation, November 8, 2010, available at https://www.heritage.org/education/report/school-choice-canada-lessons-america

47 Ibid.

48 Barbara Arrowsmith Young, *The Woman Who Changed Her Brain* (New York, NY: Free Press, 2012), pp. 49-50.

49 Ibid, p. 50.

50 Ibid.

51 Ibid.

52 Ibid, pp. 50-51.

53 Ibid, p. 51.

54 Ibid.

55 See http://achievereading.com/The_Slingerland_Approach.html

56 See http://www.normandoidge.com/?page_id=1259

57 See https://arrowsmithschool.org/eaton-arrowsmith-school-vancouver/

58 See https://www.synapseschool.org/about-us/mission-philosophy

59 See https://www.goodreads.com/quotes/57598-there-is-nothing-which-i-dread-so-much-as-a

60 See https://www.designtechhighschool.org/about-intro

61 Kerry McDonald, *Unschooled: Raising Curious, Well-Educated Children Outside the Conventional Classroom* (Chicago, IL: Chicago Review Press, 2019), pp. xvi-xvii.

62 Ibid, p. 2.

63 Ibid, p. 3.

64 Lance Izumi, *Choosing Diversity: How Charter Schools Promote Diverse Learning Models and Meet the Diverse Needs of Parents and Children* (San Francisco, CA: Pacific Research Institute, 2019), p. 26.

65 Ibid, p. 35.

66 Kerry McDonald, *Unschooled: Raising Curious, Well-Educated Children Outside the Conventional Classroom* (Chicago, IL: Chicago Review Press, 2019), p. 80.

67 Ibid, p. 80-81.

68 Ibid, p. 82.

69 Ibid, p. 85.

70   Ibid.

71   Ibid, p. 86.

72   See https://www.edchoice.org/school-choice/programs/gardin-er-scholarship-program/

73   See https://www.edchoice.org/school-choice/programs/gardin-er-scholarship-program/

74   Ibid.

75   Ibid. Under Florida's McKay voucher program, parents can use the voucher scholarship to pay for tuition for their special-needs children to attend private schools. The average voucher value in 2018-19 was $7,157, with 30,695 students participating.

76   Arely Burgos, "Gardiner scholarship helps children with special needs," *Naples Daily News*, September 11, 2019, available at https://www.naplesnews.com/story/opinion/contributors/2019/09/11/gardin-er-scholarship-helps-children-special-needs-opinion/2275074001/

77   Ibid.

78   Patrick Gibbons, "Gardiner Scholarship Funding Expected to Increase by $23 Million," May 10, 2019, available at https://www.redefine-donline.org/2019/05/gardiner-scholarship-funding-expected-to-in-crease-by-23-million/

79   See https://www.edchoice.org/school-choice/programs/gardin-er-scholarship-program/

80   See https://www.stepupforstudents.org/our-stories/hear-from-our-families/

81   Ibid.

82   See http://www.accessschool.net and http://www.accessschool.net/arrowsmith.html

83   See http://www.accessschool.net/arrowsmith.html

84   See http://www.accessschool.net/zach.html

85   Ibid.

86   Ibid.

87   Ibid.

88   Ibid.

89   See https://www.ces-schools.net/scholarships/

90   In an interview with one of the co-authors of this book, Barbara Arrowsmith-Young said that the Arrowsmith program charges schools $4,500 per student for the full-time program. Schools, if they are private, would then add in their costs and decide what to charge parents. She agreed that a Florida Gardiner Scholarship of $10,000 per student would cover all the expenses involved in an Arrowsmith program at a school. In exchange for the fee it charges schools, the Arrowsmith program provides the cognitive programs, the pre- and post-assessments, tracking, and ongoing professional development sessions. Initial teacher training has a separate fee. The program emphasizes quality control because student outcomes are dependent on the way the exercises are administered. She says: "I can't drive the point home more clearly as far as quality control is concerned because the teachers that are trained have to be diligent because without that

diligence in administrating the program properly, you will not see progress." Further: "And we track all of the data, like we have built in all these algorithms, these benchmarks, and teachers love it. If you saw the tablet, oh my gosh, the teachers walk around with the tablet and they can click on Johnny and see all of Johnny's data."

About the Authors

MIA GIORDANO

Mia Giordano is a senior at Design Tech High School, which is a charter school in Redwood Shores located on the Oracle corporate campus headquarters. Mia plans to major in history in college. She is interested in pursuing a career in national security affairs. She plays competitive tennis, loves gourmet cooking, and enjoys spending time planning her next adventure.

LANCE IZUMI

Lance Izumi is Senior Director of the Center for Education at the Pacific Research Institute. He has written and produced books, studies, and films on a wide variety of education topics. Most recently, he is the author of the 2017 book *The Corrupt Classroom: Bias, Indoctrination, Violence, and Social Engineering Show Why America Needs School Choice* and the 2019 book *Choosing Diversity: How Charter Schools Promote Diverse Learning Models and Meet the Diverse Needs of Parents and Children.*

From 2004 to 2015, he served as a member of the Board of Governors of the California Community Colleges, the largest system of higher education in the nation, and served two terms as president of the Board.

From 2015 to 2018, Lance chaired the board of directors of the Foundation for California Community Colleges, the official non-profit that supports the community college system, and remains a member of the board.

Lance served as a commissioner on the California Post-secondary Education Commission and as a member of the United States Civil Rights Commission's California Advisory Committee.

Lance received his juris doctorate from the University of Southern California School of Law, his master of arts in political science from the University of California at Davis, and his bachelor of arts in economics and history from the University of California at Los Angeles.

Acknowledgements

Many people assisted in the preparation of this book. The authors would like to thank: Christine Zanello, who was so integral to this project in so many ways and whose love for Mia is unbounded; Barbara Arrowsmith-Young for her time and critical input, plus her pioneering contributions to addressing the needs of those with brain-based learning disabilities; Dr. Greg Rose for his time and expertise, plus his important ongoing research on the Arrowsmith Program; Dr. Lauren Geary for her critical scientific advice; Kelly Ferreira for her time and recollections; Dr. Anne Weisman for her time, expertise, and recollections; Brandi Jordania Goldberg for her advice and counsel; Claire Goss for her time, expertise, and recollections; Ryan Dawson for his time and recollections; and Kerry McDonald for her time and expertise. The co-author photograph is by Tom Dawdy.

The authors would also like to thank Pacific Research Institute president and CEO Sally Pipes, PRI senior vice president Rowena Itchon, and PRI communications director Tim Anaya for editing this book (any remaining errors or omissions are the sole responsibility of the authors), graphic designer Dana Beigel, PRI vice president of development Ben Smithwick, and the other dedicated PRI staff who made this book possible.

The authors of this book worked independently. Their views and conclusions do not necessarily represent those of the board, supporters, and staff of PRI.

About Pacific
Research Institute

The Pacific Research Institute (PRI) champions freedom, opportunity, and personal responsibility by advancing free-market policy solutions. It provides practical solutions for the policy issues that impact the daily lives of all Americans, and demonstrates why the free market is more effective than the government at providing the important results we all seek: good schools, quality health care, a clean environment, and a robust economy.

Founded in 1979 and based in San Francisco, PRI is a non-profit, non-partisan organization supported by private contributions. Its activities include publications, public events, media commentary, community leadership, legislative testimony, and academic outreach.

Center for Business and Economics

PRI shows how the entrepreneurial spirit—the engine of economic growth and opportunity—is stifled by onerous taxes, regulations, and lawsuits. It advances policy reforms that promote a robust economy, consumer choice, and innovation.

Center for Education

PRI works to restore to all parents the basic right to choose the best educational opportunities for their children. Through research and grassroots outreach, PRI promotes parental choice in education, high academic standards, teacher quality, charter schools, and school-finance reform.

Center for the Environment

PRI reveals the dramatic and long-term trend toward a cleaner, healthier environment. It also examines and promotes the essential ingredients for abundant resources and environmental quality: property rights, markets, local action, and private initiative.

Center for Health Care

PRI demonstrates why a single-payer Canadian model would be detrimental to the health care of all Americans. It proposes market-based reforms that would improve affordability, access, quality, and consumer choice.

Center for California Reform

The Center for California Reform seeks to reinvigorate California's entrepreneurial self-reliant traditions. It champions solutions in education, business, and the environment that work to advance prosperity and opportunity for all the state's residents.

Center for Medical Economics and Innovation

The Center for Medical Economics and Innovation aims to educate policymakers, regulators, health care professionals, the media, and the public on the critical role that new technologies play in improving health and accelerating economic growth.